www.ingramcontent.com/pod-product-compliance
Lightning Source LLC
Chambersburg PA
CBHW041551220426
43666CB00002B/33

THE ROSENSTEIN HAGGADAH

THE ROSENSTEIN HAGGADAH

SHOSHANA SILBERMAN
Editor

MORDECHAI ROSENSTEIN
Illustrator

ibooks

new york
Habent Sua Fata Libelli

A Publication of Ibooks

Copyright © 2018 Ibooks
Illustrations Copyright © 2018 By Mordechai Rosenstein

Cover Illustration Copyright © 2018 By Mordechai Rosenstein

All rights reserved, including the right to reproduce this book or portions thereof in any form whatever.

Isbn 13: 978-1-59687-539-5

J. Boylston & Company, Publishers
Manhasset House
Shelter Island Heights, New York 11965
212-427-7139
Bricktower@Aol.com

About The Editor

In my career as a Jewish Educator, I have been a teacher, principal, and a leader of teacher training workshops across North America. I was also a consultant for the Auerbach Central Agency for Jewish Education in the Philadelphia area.

Although I wrote numerous articles for journals and newspapers, I never considered writing a book until parents at the Jewish Centre in Princeton pressed me to create a Haggadah with features that did not exist at the time. In 1987, *A Family Haggadah* (geared to multi-age participants) was published, and I became an "accidental" best selling author. A decade later, *A Family Haggadah II* (for families with older children or just adults) was published, and over the years more than a million copies of these two Haggadot were sold.

I then turned to writing other books that seemed to fill a need, especially in family education, including: *The Whole Megillah (Almost)*, *Tiku Shofar: A High Holiday Mahzor for Students and Families*, *Siddur Shema Yisrael: A Shabbat Family Prayerbook*, and *Family Rhymes for Jewish Times*. I also had my first story, *The Wall*, published, as well as a curriculum on modern slavery.

However, I never lost my fascination and deep love for Haggadot. In 2006, I had the incredible opportunity to write the *Jewish World Family Haggadah*, with the amazing photographer Zion Ozeri. Now I have the privilege of creating a new Haggadah with renowned artist Mordechai Rosenstein, whose work I have long admired and collected. I hope *The Rosenstein Haggadah* will enable participants to engage in a lively and meaningful Seder experience, where both text and paintings facilitate a spiritual journey.

Shoshana Silberman

Dr. Shoshana Silberman holds a B.S. degree from Columbia University, a B.H.L. from Gratz College, an M.S.T. from the University of Chicago and an Ed.D from Temple University.

Dr. Shoshana Silberman can be reached at shoshanamsilberman@gmail.com for speaking engagements and writing projects.

About The Artist

The story of the Jewish People's exodus from Egypt culminates in the splitting of the Sea of Reeds and our ancestors passing through it on dry land. This is a tremendous testament to the power and significance of the space in-between. As the waters of the sea stood as walls to guide them, it was the dry land, the space in-between, which facilitated the new nation's safe passage. Similarly, the Kabbalah teaches that the space between the letters of the Hebrew alphabet, the abstract forms that bind them one to another, have meaning and significance as well.

That thought is one that resonated with me since my youth. I remember as a child growing up in Philadelphia, I would study the form of the Hebrew letters and the spaces between them within the Daily Forward newspaper, sitting open on the kitchen table. That fascination only grew stronger as I attended and graduated in the first class of Akiba Hebrew Academy, as well as through my formal training at the Philadelphia College of Art and nine years working as a textile designer in New York City. It was during my time in art school that I studied with leading Abstract Expressionist Franz Kline, whose mastery of black and white, echoed the Kabbalah's recognition that every area of the artist's canvas is important to the whole: one defines and explains the other.

Today, over fifty years since I returned to Philadelphia, I still love translating the abstract shapes of the Hebrew alphabet, adding vitality to the letters and connecting spaces. I have been privileged to travel all over the world, creating, and displaying unique pieces of art that now beautify homes, synagogues, and communal spaces.

As you consider the desire for and value of freedom that is highlighted throughout the Haggadah, I invite you to fully experience the freedom of movement contained in the Hebrew letters themselves. And just as we recognize tonight the significance of the unbroken link to the people and events described herein, I hope that the abstract space that serves to link the letters one to the other will provide avenues for discussion and will enhance your Seder experience.

Mordechai Rosenstein

Signed and numbered editions of all images contained in this Haggadah are available through Mordechai Rosenstein's agent, Barry Magen, c/o Rosenstein Arts, LLC. To see more of Mordechai's art, visit his website, rosensteinarts.com.

Dedication

This Haggadah is dedicated to the memory of my beloved husband Mel (zl"), my true love, who was always a source of strength and inspiration to our family. It also honors the memory of my dear parents, Samuel Ribner and Betty Ribner Borok and my brother Elliot. It honors my "treasures", children Shmuel, Lisa and Gabriel, son–in law Daniel, and daughters–in-law Sara and Alison, as well as my amazing grandchildren: Noam, Jonah, Yaakov, Adira, Meir, and Devorah. May they carry on the family tradition of lively and engaging Sedarim, where all is discussed respectfully "in the name of heaven" and sung with enthusiasm and great joy.

Shoshana Silberman

I would like to dedicate this Haggadah to my wife and companion of fifty-five years, Mati, whose constant faith in my ability as a creative artist has been the most important element in my career.

Mordechai Rosenstein

The following is the dedication at the beginning of a third Seder created by the Young Peoples League, an organization that was affiliated with the United Synagogue of America, (now the United Synagogue for Conservative Judaism), for which my father, Samuel Ribner, was a president and subequent director. It followed the United Nations vote to establish the State of Israel, and then the declaration of war declared by six Arab states - Egypt, Syria, Jordan, Iraq, Saudi Arabia, and Lebanon.

Today, all Jewry is aligned against the forces of oppression. Having granted our brethren freedom in the Holy Land, we pray to God that the United Nations will reaffirm their decision with courage and strength, so that peace may be again enjoyed by the peoples of the world. To our heroic fellow Jews who are now engaged in the defense of the Jewish State, as well as the Jewish people, who are once again seeking liberty and freedom for all Israel, we of the Y.P. L. dedicate this Seder service. Theirs is a dedication of loyalty, of freedom and of truth. May we be worthy of their sacrifice.

As so many have done before us, may we be inspired to work for freedom, equality and peace, for us and for all humanity.

Shoshana Silberman

Introduction

The Rosenstein Haggadah, edited by Shoshana Silberman, features the unique and captivating artwork of acclaimed artist Modechai Rosenstein. As you recite the ancient text, feast your eyes on the paintings, for they will provide a message of freedom, joy and redemption.

Shoshana Silberman has provided commentaries old and new, Ashkenazic and Sephardic, traditional and liberal, male and female, original and learned. It celebrates *Clal Yisrael* – all Israel.

The Haggadah text has been supplemented not only with commentaries, but also discussion questions, activities and songs to make the Seder engaging to multi-generational participants. The section entitled, *Creating a More Lively Seder* is geared to all ages, but especially the children.

Titles and explanations of paintings can be found at the end of this Haggadah in a section called Art Notes.

HOW BEST TO USE THIS HAGGADAH

If you are serving as leader or co-leader of your Seder, it is vital to read the Haggadah beforehand to become familiar with the text. Next, think about ideas and themes that seem especially appealing to you. It is also helpful to consider the needs of the participants who will be present, especially if they differ in age and background. Then select commentaries, discussion questions, and activities that you think will be stimulating and a good match (or balance) for attendees. Also, select pictures on which you would like to focus. Leave time to explore an issue fully, rather than rushing to complete every item. Leave something for next year! Even if you have a plan, leave room for spontaneity.

Plan ahead! There are a number of things to plan in advance. A list of the required and optional items you will need for your Seder preparation follows directly. Having them ready will make your Seder run smoothly and increase interest and appreciation.

Setting the Seder Table

Holiday candles

Wine or grape juice
(enough for four cups per person)

Wine cups for each person

Matzah

Seder plate

Cup for Elijah filled with wine

Three matzot
(covered)

Afikomen bag or special napkin

Pillows for reclining

Salt water or lemon juice for dipping

Cup, bowl, and towel for washing

Haggadah for each person

The Seder Plate

Beitzah	roasted egg	בֵּיצָה
Karpas	parsley, celery, or potato	כַּרְפַּס
Z'roa	roasted bone (beet or avocado seed for vegetarians	זְרוֹעַ
Charoset	Ashkenazim use chopped apples & nuts, wine & honey, flavored with cinnamon. Sephardim use chopped figs, dates, raisins, apricots or oranges, and other spices. Some Israelis add a banana.	חֲרֹסֶת
Maror	bitter herb (usually horseradish)	מָרוֹר
Chazeret	usually romaine lettuce (for the Hillel sandwich)	חֲזֶרֶת

Optional Seder Items

(Below are other items you might use or prepare for your Seder.
More details about them are provided throughout this Haggadah.)

Cup for Miriam filled with water

Extra matzah for the Matzah of Hope

Flowers for the table

Individual Seder plates

Olives as a symbol of peace
(The olive branch is a universal symbol of peace, associated with the dove in the story of
Noah and the ark. Olives can be served after the hard-boiled eggs, prior to the meal.)

An orange as a symbol of inclusion[1]

Scallions to use during Dayenu

Hard-boiled eggs for all participants (served prior to the meal)

Afikomen gifts

Seder Trivia Game

Duplicated Passover story, cut in sections

Cups numbered 1,2,3 and 4 to indicate which cup of wine is being blessed

Pictures of frogs, stuffed animals or plastic frogs

Echad Mi Yodea "certificates"
(for knowing all the answers to the song)

Puppets or pictures for Chad Gadya

Omer Calendar
(for counting the days of the Omer)

Omer Tzedakah Box
(for giving tzedakah during the time of Omer)

A "kittel" (a white robe), worn traditionally by the Seder leader
(Wearing a kittel has various interpretations. The color white signifies freedom; the robe
reminds us of the Temple service offered at Passover by the priests who wore special robes.
The kittel is associated with purity and reminds us of the sacredness of life.)

THE ROSENSTEIN HAGGADAH

CREATING A MORE LIVELY SEDER

"Only the lesson which is enjoyed can be learned well."
Talmud Avodah Zara 10:A

This section provides a variety of ways to make your Seder lively so that real and meaningful learning occurs. What follows are ideas and suggestions for you to do before or during the Seder. Read the list each year and select ones that you think would work for your family and guests. The goal is to have participants of all ages, as well as multi-stages of knowledge regarding the Haggadah, be engaged with the Seder.

* Set the tone for the holiday by donating non-perishable food to a food bank. Make a contribution to an organization that provides kosher for Passover food to needy Jewish families. (Your local rabbi can be helpful with this.)

* Create a chametz checklist for children to clean out their rooms and their school bags before Pesach.

* Plan a family trip to a local car wash to clean and vacuum your car/s.[2]

Add a magnifying glass to the spoon and feather used to search for chametz, so young children can become "chametz detectives." as they search."[3]

* Send a package of Passover foods and Haggadot to college students who may not have access to a Seder, or just would enjoy some holiday treats.

* We add to the joy of the holiday by inviting guests to the Seder. It is a mitzvah to invite newcomers to the community, college students away from home, or anyone who might be alone. Your children might like to invite a family that includes school or neighborhood friends.

* Decide in advance who will be the leader of the Seder. He or she can invite participants to share explanations or commentaries for items on the Seder Plate, or different parts of the Seder.

* In order to make the Seder Plate more beautiful, purchase a fresh horseradish about three weeks prior to Pesach. Cut the heavy, knot-like head off, making it about one inch high. Place it in a shallow saucepan, with a little water. Replenish the water daily. This will force the horseradish to sprout with lovely green shoots.[4] Even from bitterness, we can grow hope for the future!

* Parsley can be grown indoors after Purim to be used at the Seder.

* Involve children in activities such as preparing charoset and setting the table. Try recipes for both Sephardic and Ashkenazic charoset, or ones popular in Israel. All can be found on the internet.

* Prepare a large tray with a variety of cut up vegetables for everyone to nosh after the blessing for karpas is recited. This will help stave off hunger until the meal begins.

* Use the decorations children have made at preschool or religious school to create excitement about the Seder. Or, make some at home (e.g. matzah cover, bag for 10 plagues, decorative cups for Elijah and Miriam, paper flowers, pictures for each section of the Haggadah and afikomen bag.)

* Some families use sheets or blankets to turn their Seder space into a tent. The Seder Plate can be placed on a low table, and participants can sit on the floor with pillows, to feel like they are in the Middle East. Suggest wearing costumes, as well.

* Have older children or teens create maps to show the route of the Exodus.

* Follow the Yemenite tradition of turning the entire Seder table into one large Seder Plate, with a border of parsley leaves stacked along the edges.[5]

* Prior to the Seder, involve older children or teens by encouraging them to compare the film The Prince of Egypt (or even the 1956 film, The Ten Commandments) with the Torah text of the Exodus story. What's similar? What's different? What additions or changes did they like or dislike?

* Older children or teens can make a short video of a scene from the Exodus story using a cell phone.

* Have younger children create a "Kiddush Countdown" by drawing, cutting out, and coloring four paper cups of wine. Label the cups 1 - 4. Children can hold up the appropriate number when that cup of wine is blessed.[6]

* Make a chart that lists the steps of the Seder. Use Hebrew and/or English, as well as pictures for the younger ones. Children can be invited to come up to the chart and move a clothespin to indicate the appropriate step in the Seder.[7]

* Write each step of the Seder on a colorful piece of 8x11 paper. Use a jump rope, attaching the papers in order with a clothespin, for each step.

* Create hand motions for each step of the Seder. Children can do them when the Order of the Seder is recited or sung.

* In many Sephardic homes, an elder would dress in costume, pretending that he left Egypt and would describe the miracles he saw there.[8] Ask someone with talent and inclination to do this at your Seder.

* The Prague Haggadah of 1526 includes a picture of a man walking with a satchel on his shoulder, next to the verse, "…So did our ancestors go, with their kneading bowls wrapped in their cloaks." (Exodus 12:14) Some enactment of leaving in haste was part of many Sedarim in both Sephardic and Ashkenazic households.[9] Create your own enactment.

* Make puppets for the children to use for the Maggid section, or prepare props to help tell the story.

* Choose people to role-play a talk show host, who is interviewing characters from the Pesach story.

* Have participants take turns playing a Pesach Twenty Questions game. Use characters in the Pesach story as a theme. Write the names of the characters on 8x11 sheets of paper with a marker, so the rest of the group can answer yes or no, when the volunteer asks questions.

* Ask older children to create a trivia quiz for younger ones.

* Create the Rebellion! This might be a perfect assignment for teens. Give participants information about the rabbis who were present, as well as information about the Bar Kochba rebellion against the Romans in 132-135 CE. They can give a presentation when the section on B'nai B'rak is read.[10]

* Another activity for teens would be to seek out Passover songs on the internet to lead at the Seder. They can be real songs about freedom, (e.g. *Oh Freedom* or *If I Had A Hammer*) or parodies taken from Broadway shows or pop culture. Challenge them to create a song themselves.

* Before the Seder, ask a guest who is in business, and/or one who is a psychologist, to prepare an analysis of the negotiations between Moses and Pharaoh.

* Duplicate the story of the Exodus (using excerpts from the Bible, or your own version, or simply use the one in this Haggadah.) Cut up the story and randomly give out parts. Have each participant read when it is appropriate.

* Before the Seder, tear pieces of paper in two, but in a random fashion, like a puzzle. On one half, write a question about the Exodus story and on the other half, write the answer. Or, simply write matched pairs of Passover words, (e.g. "Hillel" and "sandwich.") Mix and then distribute the questions and answers or word pairs. Have participants find their match. They will know if their answers are correct, if the torn sheets

of paper match (like the broken afikomen.) This activity, will not only help get the discussion about Maggid started, but will also provide a good stretch for young and old.

* Prepare a Passover Jeopardy Game. Write down the questions in advance. You may play rounds of Jeopardy throughout the Seder, or play a longer game as part of the Maggid.

* In some homes the leader hides the afikomen and the children search for it to receive a reward. In other homes, the children hide it and return it for a "ransom." Decide beforehand, which way you'd like to do it, or do it the first way the first night and the second way the second night.

* Create an Afikomen Scavenger Hunt that will lead the children to the afikomen. Encourage the children to decide together on a charity to donate the prize money in lieu of (or in addition to) receiving a gift, thus extending the Haggadah's message of social justice into our day.[11]

* To help children find the afikomen, give clues when they are "hot or cold" depending on whether they are near or far from the hidden afikomen. You could also sing a song loudly when they are near the hidden afikomen or softly when they are far from it.

* Have an Echad Mi Yodeah Contest. Create certificates for all those who can answer, Who knows one? Who knows two? etc.

* Assign characters in the Chad Gadya song to the children and "young at heart." When the verse with their character is mentioned, they should make a sound that corresponds to their assigned character.

* Have the children create Chad Gadya sock puppets to act out the song.

* It was customary in Eastern Europe to give the children some nuts on the nights of the Sedarim. This treat (in their shells) is also perfect for playing games such as the following:

- Guessing which hand the nut was put
- Guessing if there are an even or odd number of nuts in a hand
- Guessing how many nuts are in a large jar
- Nut pitching into a bowl or bag.[12]

* Have children create a special calendar for counting the omer. It could include inspirational verses from *Pirkei Avot*, and/or suggestions for doing mitzvot (e.g. making a quilt from material scraps to donate to an appropriate charity.) A special tzedakah box can be made to collect money each night of the omer (except chagim and Shabbat.)

* Agree to do a family tzedakah or chesed project during Chol HaMoed Pesach (the intermediate days of Passover.) For example: Bring Passover treats to a nursing home and sing some of the Seder songs for the residents. Contribute to an organization that works for freedom and equality.

* Rejoice in "Chag Aviv" (the holiday of spring.) Plan to visit an arboretum or park with gardens. Fly a kite – a wonderful symbol of freedom.

* To enhance next year's Seder, select a craft project to do during the time of Chol HaMoed or right after the festival.

Plant Righteousness For Yourselves; Harvest The Fruits Of Goodness.
Hosea 10:12

Lighting the Festival Candles

Before sunset, we light the festival candles and recite this blessing:
(*On Shabbat, we add the words in brackets*)

בָּרוּךְ אַתָּה יי אֱלֹהֵינוּ מֶלֶךְ הָעוֹלָם אֲשֶׁר קִדְּשָׁנוּ בְּמִצְוֹתָיו וְצִוָּנוּ לְהַדְלִיק נֵר שֶׁל (שַׁבָּת וְשֶׁל) יוֹם טוֹב.

Baruch Atah Adonai, Eloheinu melech haolam, asher kid'shanu b'mitzvotav v'tzivanu l'hadlik ner shel [Shabat v'shel] Yom Tov.

Blessed are You, Adonai our God, Sovereign of the world, who made us holy by Your mitzvot, and commanded us to light the [Shabbat and] festival lights.

בָּרוּךְ אַתָּה יי אֱלֹהֵינוּ מֶלֶךְ הָעוֹלָם, שֶׁהֶחֱיָנוּ וְקִיְּמָנוּ וְהִגִּיעָנוּ לַזְּמַן הַזֶּה.

Baruch Atah Adonai, Eloheinu melech haolam, shehecheyanu, v'kiy'manu, v'higiyanu, lazman hazeh.

Blessed are You, Adonai our God, Sovereign of the world, who has kept us alive and sustained us, so we can reach this special occasion.

The Order of the Seder

Jews around the world follow the same order of the Seder. The Seder contains fourteen parts that we recite in order.

(If you read or sing the words for the order of the Seder in Hebrew, you will see that it is a rhyme. This is a mnemonic device to help us remember what comes next. To introduce each section of the Seder, read or sing the song, but only to that part.)

KADESH	Sanctifying the wine	קַדֵּשׁ
UR'CHATZ	Washing our hands	וּרְחַץ
KARPAS	Dipping a vegetable in salt water	כַּרְפַּס
YACHATZ	Breaking the middle matzah; Hiding the larger half	יַחַץ
MAGGID	Telling the story	מַגִּיד
RACHTZAH	Washing (with a blessing)	רָחְצָה
MOTZI MATZAH	Eating Matzah	מוֹצִיא מַצָּה
MAROR	Dipping the Bitter Herb	מָרוֹר
KORECH	Eating the Hillel sandwich	כּוֹרֵךְ
SHULCAN ORECH	Eating the Meal	שֻׁלְחָן עוֹרֵךְ
TZAFUN	Tasting the Afikomen	צָפוּן
BARECH	Blessing after the Meal	בָּרֵךְ
HALLEL	Singing Songs of Praise	הַלֵּל
NIRTZAH	Concluding the Seder	נִרְצָה

Seder Warm-ups

Have participants recall favorite memories of Sedarim past.
Stop to remember who may be missing from your Seder this year.
Share special memories of that person/s.
Acknowledge who is at the Seder for the first time.

ברוך אתה
יי אלהינו
מלך העולם

KADESH

SAY THE KIDDUSH

First Cup – "I Will Take You Out"

(Fill the cups with wine.)

We are now ready for the first cup of wine, which we drink while reclining.
[On Shabbat add the words in brackets.]

(וַיְהִי עֶרֶב וַיְהִי בֹקֶר יוֹם הַשִּׁשִּׁי,
וַיְכֻלּוּ הַשָּׁמַיִם וְהָאָרֶץ וְכָל-צְבָאָם: וַיְכַל אֱלֹהִים בַּיּוֹם הַשְּׁבִיעִי, מְלַאכְתּוֹ אֲשֶׁר עָשָׂה,
וַיִּשְׁבֹּת בַּיּוֹם הַשְּׁבִיעִי, מִכָּל-מְלַאכְתּוֹ אֲשֶׁר עָשָׂה: וַיְבָרֶךְ אֱלֹהִים אֶת-יוֹם הַשְּׁבִיעִי,
וַיְקַדֵּשׁ אֹתוֹ, כִּי בוֹ שָׁבַת מִכָּל-מְלַאכְתּוֹ, אֲשֶׁר-בָּרָא אֱלֹהִים לַעֲשׂוֹת:)

[Vay'hi erev, vay'hi voker yom hashishi: Vay'chulu hashamayim v'ha'aretz v'chol tz'va'am. Vay'chal Elohim bayom hash'vi'i m'lachto asher asah. Vayishbot bayom hash'vi'i mikol m'lachto asher asah. Vay'varech Elohim et yom hash'vi'i vay'kadesh oto, ki vo shavat mikol m'lachto asher bara Elohim la'asot.]

[On the sixth day, the heavens and earth were finished. On the seventh day, God completed the work of creation. God blessed the seventh day and called it holy, because on that day, God rested from all the work of creation.]

בָּרוּךְ אַתָּה יְיָ, אֱלֹהֵינוּ מֶלֶךְ הָעוֹלָם, בּוֹרֵא פְּרִי הַגָּפֶן:

Blessed are You, Adonai our God, Sovereign of the world, who creates the fruit of the vine.

בָּרוּךְ אַתָּה יְיָ, אֱלֹהֵינוּ מֶלֶךְ הָעוֹלָם, אֲשֶׁר בָּחַר בָּנוּ מִכָּל-עָם, וְרוֹמְמָנוּ מִכָּל-לָשׁוֹן, וְקִדְּשָׁנוּ בְּמִצְוֹתָיו, וַתִּתֶּן-לָנוּ יְיָ אֱלֹהֵינוּ בְּאַהֲבָה (שַׁבָּתוֹת לִמְנוּחָה וּ)מוֹעֲדִים לְשִׂמְחָה, חַגִּים וּזְמַנִּים לְשָׂשׂוֹן אֶת-יוֹם (הַשַּׁבָּת הַזֶּה וְאֶת-יוֹם) חַג הַמַּצּוֹת הַזֶּה. זְמַן חֵרוּתֵנוּ, (בְּאַהֲבָה,) מִקְרָא קֹדֶשׁ, זֵכֶר לִיצִיאַת מִצְרָיִם. כִּי בָנוּ בָחַרְתָּ וְאוֹתָנוּ קִדַּשְׁתָּ מִכָּל-הָעַמִּים. (וְשַׁבָּת) וּמוֹעֲדֵי קָדְשֶׁךָ (בְּאַהֲבָה וּבְרָצוֹן) בְּשִׂמְחָה וּבְשָׂשׂוֹן הִנְחַלְתָּנוּ. בָּרוּךְ אַתָּה יְיָ, מְקַדֵּשׁ (הַשַּׁבָּת וְ)יִשְׂרָאֵל וְהַזְּמַנִּים:

Baruch Atah Adonai, Eloheinu melech haolam, asher bachar banu mikol am. V'rom'manu mikol lashon, v'kidshanu b'mitzvotav. Vatiten lanu Adonai Eloheinu, b'ahava [Shabbat limnucha u'] mo'adim l'simchah, chagim uz'manim l'sasson. Et yom [haShabbat hazeh v'et yom] chag hamatzot hazeh, z'man cherutenu, [b'ahava] mikra kodesh, zecher l'tziat Mitzrayim Ki vanu vaharta, v'otanu kidashta mikol ha'amim [v'Shabbat] u'mo'adei kadsh'cha [b'ahava] uv'ratzon, b'simcha uv' sasson hinchaltanu. Baruch Atah Adonai, mikadesh [haShabbat v'] Yisrael, v'hazmanim.

Blessed are You, Adonai our God, Sovereign of the world, who has made us holy through Your mitzvot, and has lovingly given us the gift of [Shabbat for rest and] festivals for gladness. You have given us [Shabbat and] this Festival of Matzot, celebrations of our freedom, a holy time to recall the Exodus from Egypt. Blessed are You Adonai, who makes holy [Shabbat] the people Israel and the festivals.

(On Saturday night, add Havdalah. Note: Passover extends the spirit of Shabbat, so the blessing for the spices is not recited. The blessing for the light is said over the festival candles and not over a Havdalah candle.)

Havdalah

בָּרוּךְ אַתָּה יְיָ, אֱלֹהֵינוּ מֶלֶךְ הָעוֹלָם, בּוֹרֵא מְאוֹרֵי הָאֵשׁ:

Baruch Atah Adonai, Eloheinu melech haolam, borei m'orei ha'esh.

Blessed are You, Adonai our God, Sovereign of the world, Creator of light.

בָּרוּךְ אַתָּה יְיָ, אֱלֹהֵינוּ מֶלֶךְ הָעוֹלָם, הַמַּבְדִּיל בֵּין קֹדֶשׁ לְחֹל בֵּין אוֹר לְחֹשֶׁךְ, בֵּין יִשְׂרָאֵל לָעַמִּים, בֵּין יוֹם הַשְּׁבִיעִי לְשֵׁשֶׁת יְמֵי הַמַּעֲשֶׂה. בֵּין קְדֻשַּׁת שַׁבָּת לִקְדֻשַּׁת יוֹם טוֹב הִבְדַּלְתָּ. וְאֶת-יוֹם הַשְּׁבִיעִי מִשֵּׁשֶׁת יְמֵי הַמַּעֲשֶׂה קִדַּשְׁתָּ. הִבְדַּלְתָּ וְקִדַּשְׁתָּ אֶת-עַמְּךָ יִשְׂרָאֵל בִּקְדֻשָּׁתֶךָ. בָּרוּךְ אַתָּה יְיָ, הַמַּבְדִּיל בֵּין קֹדֶשׁ לְקֹדֶשׁ:

THE ROSENSTEIN HAGGADAH

Blessed are You, Adonai our God, Sovereign of the world, who separates holy from the profane, light from darkness, Israel from the nations, and Shabbat from the six days of creation. Blessed are You, Adonai, who separates the holiness of Shabbat from the holiness of the festivals.

(continue with the Shehecheyanu prayer)

בָּרוּךְ אַתָּה יְיָ, אֱלֹהֵינוּ מֶלֶךְ הָעוֹלָם, שֶׁהֶחֱיָנוּ וְקִיְּמָנוּ וְהִגִּיעָנוּ לַזְּמַן הַזֶּה:

Baruch Atah Adonai, Eloheinu melech haolam, shehecheyanu, v'ky'manu, v'higiyanu, lazman hazeh.

Blessed are You, Adonai our God, Sovereign of the world, who has kept us alive and sustained us, so that we can reach this special occasion.

(All drink the wine while reclining.)

The kiddush includes the words, *sasson* and *simcha*, (gladness and joy.) In Chassidic teaching, the word gladness refers to our happiness over a redemption that we have experienced (the Exodus from Egypt.) The word joy refers to a future promise – the Messianic redemption. It is important to note that the theme of both past and future redemptions will occur throughout the Haggadah text.

During the Seder, we drink four cups of wine, which represent God's four promises to the people of Israel. (Exodus 6:6-7)

First Cup   "I will take you out."

Second Cup   "I will rescue you."

Third Cup   "I will redeem you."

Fourth Cup   "I will take you to be my people."

Some associate the four cups of wine with the four matriarchs of Israel – Sarah, Rebecca, Leah, and Rachel. What are characteristics that you associate with each matriarch? Do you have a favorite one?

THE ROSENSTEIN HAGGADAH

UR'CHATZ

יְרְחַץ

WASH OUR HANDS

As the priests in the Holy Temple were commanded to wash, we wash to symbolize that our actions must be of service to God.

(Take a cup of water in one hand and pour it over the other, then reverse hands. You can do this ritual at a sink or bring a cup, bowl, and towel to the table. No blessing is recited.)

...THE WATERS WERE SPLIT. exodus 14:21

KARPAS

בַּרְפַּס

DIP A GREEN VEGETABLE

(Distribute the green vegetable.)

We dip a green vegetable into the salt water and recite this blessing:

בָּרוּךְ אַתָּה יְיָ, אֱלֹהֵינוּ מֶלֶךְ הָעוֹלָם, בּוֹרֵא פְּרִי הָאֲדָמָה:

Baruch Atah Adonai, Eloheinu melech haolam, borei p'ri ha'adamah.
Blessed are You, Adonai our God, Sovereign of the world, who creates the fruit of the earth.

(All eat the green vegetable.)

The karpas is usually parsley or celery. In Eastern Europe, potatoes were used, as they were more available.

In ancient times, like today, an appetizer was served at festive occasions to whet the appetite for the meal to come. On Pesach, we whet our appetites to eat the required amount of matzah later in the Seder.

We dip the karpas into the salt water to remember the tears our ancestors shed when they were slaves.

Passover is the springtime of the year, the season of renewal. This timing is reflected in Song of Songs 2:10-12.

"Arise my beloved; come away my fairest. For the winter is past, the rains are over and gone. Blossoms have appeared in the land; the time of singing has come."

Some view the Song of Songs as a spring love poem. Others view it as an allegory of the relationship between God and the people Israel. As you pass around the Karpas, sing "Dodi Li," a love song from the Song of Songs or your own favorite love song.

דּוֹדִי לִי וַאֲנִי לוֹ, הָרֹעֶה בַּשּׁוֹשַׁנִּים.
מִי זֹאת עוֹלָה מִן הַמִּדְבָּר, מְקֻטֶּרֶת מוֹר וּלְבוֹנָה.

Dodi li va'ani lo, haro'eh bashoshanim. (2x)
Mi zot olah min hamidbar, mi zot olah,
M'kuteret mor, mor u'levonan, mor u'levonan?

"My beloved is mine and I am his.
Who is she coming from the desert, in clouds of myrrh and frankincense?"

Song of Songs 2:16; 3-6

YAHATZ

BREAK THE MIDDLE MATZAH

First, we break the middle matzah into two pieces. Then we wrap the larger piece, the afikomen or dessert matzah, and set it aside. Next, we return the smaller piece to the place with the other two matzot.

(Uncover the matzah plate and raise it for all present to see.)

הָא לַחְמָא עַנְיָא דִי אֲכָלוּ אַבְהָתָנָא בְּאַרְעָא דְמִצְרָיִם. כָּל דִכְפִין יֵיתֵי וְיֵכוֹל, כָּל דִצְרִיךְ יֵיתֵי וְיִפְסַח. הָשַׁתָּא הָכָא, לְשָׁנָה הַבָּאָה בְּאַרְעָא דְיִשְׂרָאֵל. הָשַׁתָּא עַבְדֵי, לְשָׁנָה הַבָּאָה בְּנֵי חוֹרִין:

Ha lachma anya di achalu avhatana b'ara d'Mitzraim. Kol dichfin yeitei v'yechol. Kol ditzrich yeitei v'yifsach. Hashatah hacha lashana haba'ah b'ara d' Yisrael. Hashatah avdei l'shanah haba'ah b'nai chorin.

This is the very bread of poverty that our ancestors ate in the land of Egypt. Let all who are hungry come and eat. Let all who are needy come and celebrate Passover with us. Now we celebrate here. Next year, may we celebrate in the land of Israel. Next year, may we be truly free.

(Fill the wine cups for the second time.)

This is the very bread of poverty...

We break the middle matzah to show that our redemption is not complete.

In Ashkenazic tradition, there are three matzot at the Seder to represent the Priests, the Levites, and the Israelites. A Sephardic interpretation is that the top matzah represents *thought*, the middle matzah *speech*, and the bottom matzah *action*. Speech is placed in the middle to show that it should be linked to our thoughts and actions.[13]

Sephardic and Mizrachi Jews often put the afikomen in a sock or napkin, which is given to a child who slings it over his or her shoulder. The leader then asks, "From where did you come?" The child answers, "From Egypt." The leader then asks, "Where are you going?" The child replies, "To Jerusalem." The last question is, "What are you taking with you?" The child points to the matzah.[14] In Egypt, the wrapped matzah is shifted from the right shoulder to the left shoulder when Jerusalem is mentioned as the destination.[15]

In Iraq the father would offer 100 pieces of gold to the youngest child to guard the afikomen. When the child agrees, the afikomen is tied to his or her body in a special cloth, and everyone tries to talk the child into giving it away. Of course the child does not give in to temptation.[16]

In Hungary, the leader would put the afikomen in a scarf, put it on his shoulder, stand up and say in Yiddish, "Geimir! Geimir"! ("Let's go! Let's go!") In southern Germany, leaders would say, "So sind die kinder Jisroelaux Mizraim gegangen, so war es." ("Thus did the Israelites leave Egypt, and so it was.")[17]

There is a North African custom that before reciting "Let all who are hungry…" the leader takes the Seder Plate and circles it above the head of each participant while joyfully singing the verse, "In haste we went out of Egypt." This is to indicate that life is a cycle and our fortunes change.[18]

The verses of *Ha Lachma Anya* ("This is the very bread of poverty…") are in Aramaic, the vernacular at the time they were written, to ensure that all would understand the meaning. Today, we can still recite it in Aramaic for its historic value and in our own language to emphasize its importance.

The bread of poverty is more than a symbol of the past. It conveys to us that there is still poverty and suffering in the world, which must be addressed.

An empty plate represents the homeless. They are even less fortunate than the Israelite slaves, who at least had dwelling places. We can symbolically "fill the plate" by pledging money or work hours at a soup kitchen or shelter.

If you have decided to include an orange on the Seder Plate, this is an appropriate time to point to it as a symbol of inclusion. Professor Susannah Heschel, to bring attention to the exclusion of GLBTQ people from the Jewish community, originally created this symbol. The orange suggests the fruitfulness that results when all kinds of Jews participates in Jewish communal life.

It would also be a good time to explain other optional symbols on your Seder Plate. Is there one you'd like to add?

About the Four Questions

We begin with astonishment. "Mah Nishtana?" (What has changed?) The obligation to question has no limit of age, gender, social status, or knowledge level. All are required to ask."[19]

Actually, there is just one question asked. "Why is this night different from all other nights?" Then there are four statements, giving examples of different practices.

Some translate the opening line of the Four Questions as "How different this night is from all other nights?" Which of the two translations do you prefer?

By asking the four questions, we open a doorway to further conversation. What questions do you want to discuss this year?

The first two questions are about slavery; the last two are about freedom. We must relive both the despair of slavery and the joy of freedom to fully understand and celebrate Pesach.

The Four Questions were probably written for fathers to use to explain unique aspects of the Seder. There is no record of any custom for children reciting them. It is believed that the custom came into existence in Ashkenazic circles toward the end of the seventeenth century. We want all present to listen to the Four Questions. Having children, especially the youngest, ask them, certainly gets the attention of the adults.[20]

If there are those who can recite the Four Questions in other languages, encourage them to do so.

Wicked people do not ask questions; they give answers that rationalize their beliefs.[21] Do you think this is true?

MAGGID

TELL THE STORY OF PASSOVER

The Four Questions

(Traditionally, the youngest child asks the Four Questions, but each child could do it in order of birth. Consider having the oldest adult present share the honors with the youngest.)

מַה נִּשְׁתַּנָּה הַלַּיְלָה הַזֶּה מִכָּל הַלֵּילוֹת?

שֶׁבְּכָל הַלֵּילוֹת אָנוּ אוֹכְלִין חָמֵץ וּמַצָּה.
הַלַּיְלָה הַזֶּה כֻּלּוֹ מַצָּה:

שֶׁבְּכָל הַלֵּילוֹת אָנוּ אוֹכְלִין שְׁאָר יְרָקוֹת
הַלַּיְלָה הַזֶּה מָרוֹר:

שֶׁבְּכָל הַלֵּילוֹת אֵין אָנוּ מַטְבִּילִין אֲפִילוּ פַּעַם אֶחָת.
הַלַּיְלָה הַזֶּה שְׁתֵּי פְעָמִים:

שֶׁבְּכָל הַלֵּילוֹת אָנוּ אוֹכְלִין בֵּין יוֹשְׁבִין וּבֵין מְסֻבִּין.
הַלַּיְלָה הַזֶּה כֻּלָּנוּ מְסֻבִּין:

Mah nishtana halailah hazeh mikol haleilot?
Shb'chol haleilot anu ochlin chametz u'matzah. Halaila hazeh kulo matzah.
Shb'chol haleilot anu ochlin sh'ar yerakot. Halailah hazeh maror.
Shb'chol haleilot anu matbilin afilu pa'am echat. Halaila hazeh sh'tei f'amim.
Shb'chol haleilot anu ochlin bein yoshvin u'vein mesubin. Halaila hazeh kulanu m'subin.

Why is this night different from all the other nights of the year?
On all other nights, we eat bread or matzah. On this night, we eat only matzah.
On all other nights, we eat a variety of vegetables. On this night, we must eat maror, a bitter vegetable.
On all other nights, we are not required to dip a vegetable even once. On this night, we must dip twice.
On all other nights, we eat sitting any way we like. On this night, we recline on pillows.

And God spoke to Moses.

We Were Slaves

עֲבָדִים הָיִינוּ לְפַרְעֹה בְּמִצְרָיִם. וַיּוֹצִיאֵנוּ יְיָ אֱלֹהֵינוּ מִשָּׁם, בְּיָד חֲזָקָה וּבִזְרוֹעַ נְטוּיָה, וְאִלּוּ לֹא הוֹצִיא הַקָּדוֹשׁ בָּרוּךְ הוּא אֶת־אֲבוֹתֵינוּ מִמִּצְרַיִם, הֲרֵי אָנוּ וּבָנֵינוּ וּבְנֵי בָנֵינוּ, מְשֻׁעְבָּדִים הָיִינוּ לְפַרְעֹה בְּמִצְרָיִם. וַאֲפִילוּ כֻּלָּנוּ חֲכָמִים, כֻּלָּנוּ נְבוֹנִים, כֻּלָּנוּ זְקֵנִים, כֻּלָּנוּ יוֹדְעִים אֶת־הַתּוֹרָה, מִצְוָה עָלֵינוּ לְסַפֵּר בִּיצִיאַת מִצְרָיִם. וְכָל הַמַּרְבֶּה לְסַפֵּר בִּיצִיאַת מִצְרַיִם, הֲרֵי זֶה מְשֻׁבָּח:

Avadim haiyenu, atah b'nai chorin.

Once we were slaves to the Pharaoh in Egypt and Adonai, our God, took us out, "with a mighty hand and an outstretched arm." If the Holy One of Blessing had not brought our ancestors out of Egypt, then we and our descendants would still be enslaved in Egypt. Even if we were all wise, or all full of understanding, or we were all elders who had told the story numerous times, or all Torah scholars, it is still our duty to tell the story. The more we expand upon the story, the more we are to be praised.

THE ROSENSTEIN HAGGADAH

This reading does not specifically answer the Four Questions. It is not really a narrative, but a declaration as to why we are all obligated to tell the story of the Exodus and express our gratitude for our deliverance.

When Bukkarian Jews come to *Avadim Hayinu* (We Were Slaves in Egypt), the Seder leader rises and walks around in a bent position, as if he or she were a slave. The physical demonstration helps participants imagine being a slave during the Exodus story. In the villages around Mumbai, the Bene Israel dip their hands in the blood of sheep and press them on papers, which are hung above the doorways, as a Chamsa (an amulet referencing the protective hand of God.)[21] Moroccan Jews have a similar custom, but use charoset instead of blood.[22]

What kinds of slavery are practiced today? Do you think we are moving in the direction of greater or lesser freedom in our country and throughout the world?

Children's Song

Bang and Dig

Bang! Bang! Bang!

Bang your hammers low.

Bang! Bang! Bang!

Give a heavy blow.

Chorus
Cause it's work, work, work,
every day and every night.
Cause it's work, work, work,
when it's dark and when it's light.

Dig! Dig! Dig!

Dig your shovels deep

Dig! Dig! Dig!

There's no time for sleep.

Repeat Chorus

The B'nai B'rak Story

While reading the Haggadah is mandatory, elaborating on it is praiseworthy. We are shown an example of this in the B'nai B'rak story.

An incident happened with Rabbi Eliezer, Rabbi Yehoshuah, Rabbi Elazar ben Azaria, Rabbi Akiva, and Rabbi Tarfon. They were celebrating at a Seder in B'nai B'rak and were recounting the story of the Exodus from Egypt all through the night, Their students came and interrupted them saying, "Our rabbis, the time has come for reciting the morning Shema!"

מַעֲשֶׂה בְּרַבִּי אֱלִיעֶזֶר, וְרַבִּי יְהוֹשֻׁעַ, וְרַבִּי אֶלְעָזָר בֶּן־עֲזַרְיָה, וְרַבִּי עֲקִיבָא, וְרַבִּי טַרְפוֹן, שֶׁהָיוּ מְסֻבִּין בִּבְנֵי־בְרַק, וְהָיוּ מְסַפְּרִים בִּיצִיאַת מִצְרַיִם, כָּל־אוֹתוֹ הַלַּיְלָה, עַד שֶׁבָּאוּ תַלְמִידֵיהֶם וְאָמְרוּ לָהֶם: רַבּוֹתֵינוּ, הִגִּיעַ זְמַן קְרִיאַת שְׁמַע, שֶׁל שַׁחֲרִית:

אָמַר רַבִּי אֶלְעָזָר בֶּן־עֲזַרְיָה. הֲרֵי אֲנִי כְּבֶן שִׁבְעִים שָׁנָה, וְלֹא זָכִיתִי, שֶׁתֵּאָמֵר יְצִיאַת מִצְרַיִם בַּלֵּילוֹת. עַד שֶׁדְּרָשָׁהּ בֶּן זוֹמָא. שֶׁנֶּאֱמַר: לְמַעַן תִּזְכֹּר, אֶת יוֹם צֵאתְךָ מֵאֶרֶץ מִצְרַיִם, כֹּל יְמֵי חַיֶּיךָ. יְמֵי חַיֶּיךָ הַיָּמִים. כֹּל יְמֵי חַיֶּיךָ הַלֵּילוֹת. וַחֲכָמִים אוֹמְרִים: יְמֵי חַיֶּיךָ הָעוֹלָם הַזֶּה. כֹּל יְמֵי חַיֶּיךָ לְהָבִיא לִימוֹת הַמָּשִׁיחַ:

On the night of the original Pesach, the Israelites did not sleep at all, due to the Pesach sacrifice and other preparations for their departure. One interpretation of the B'nai B'rak story is that the nightlong discussion of the Exodus by these sages was a reenactment of the Exodus.[23]

Why were these prominent rabbis in B'nai B'rak rather than at home at a Seder in their communities? Some suggest that it was a clandestine gathering to plan an uprising against Rome.

Another interpretation is that this was a mythical Seder, to heal a broken relationship between Rabbi Eliezer and the other rabbis. Rabbi Eliezer's unwillingness to accept a ruling of the High Court was the impetus for the estrangement. At this mythical Seder, all views were expressed, including Rabbi Eliezer's.

Who in the Jewish community would you say is excluded today?

"The story of Pesach never grows old, because the struggle for freedom never ends and therefore each generation adds its commentary to the old-new story."[24]

The One Who Is Everywhere

Once we worshipped idols, but now we worship God, the One Who Is Everywhere.

בָּרוּךְ הַמָּקוֹם. בָּרוּךְ הוּא.
בָּרוּךְ שֶׁנָּתַן תּוֹרָה לְעַמּוֹ יִשְׂרָאֵל. בָּרוּךְ הוּא.

Baruch HaMakom. Baruch Hu. Baruch Shenatan Torah l'amo Yisrael. Baruch Hu.

Blessed is The One Who Is Everywhere. Blessed is God. Blessed is the One who gave the Torah to the people Israel. Blessed is God.

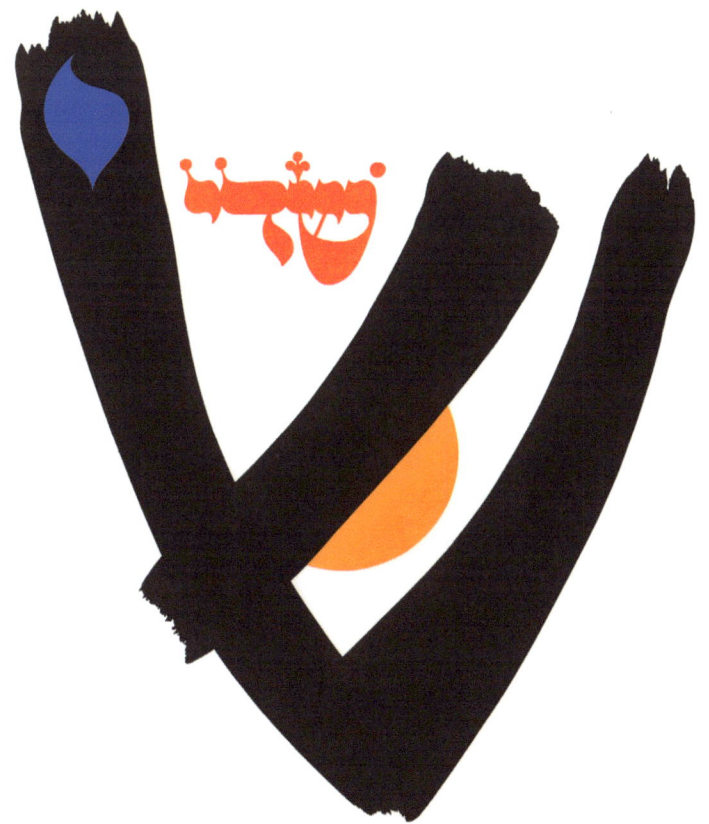

When he was five years old, Menachum Mendel of Kotsk asked his father, "Where is God"? His father replied, "God is everywhere." "No", replied the future Rebbe, "I think God is where you let God in." Where do you find God?

If God is described as *Makom* (Place), perhaps that teaches that God is a destination. Our lifelong goal is then a spiritual journey.

The Four Children

The Torah addresses itself to four children: the wise, the wicked, the simple, and one who does not know how to ask.

What does the wise child ask? "What is the meaning of the laws and rules which our God has commanded us?" (Deuteronomy 6:20) You should explain to that child all the laws of Passover, including the rule that nothing may be eaten after the afikomen.

What does the wicked child ask? "What does this service mean to you?" (Exodus 12:26) implying to you and not to him or her. Since this child excludes himself or herself from the rest of the community, you answer in a shocking manner. "I celebrate Passover because of what God did for me when I went out of Egypt." (Exodus 13:8) If the wicked child had been in Egypt, he or she would not have been included in the redemption.

What does the simple child ask? "What is this?" You answer: "With a mighty hand God took us out of Egypt, out of slavery." (Exodus 13:14)

As for the one who does not know how to ask, you must introduce the subject yourself, as it is written, "You shall tell your child on that day. It is because of what God did for me when I left Egypt." (Exodus 13:8)

כְּנֶגֶד אַרְבָּעָה בָנִים דִּבְּרָה תוֹרָה. אֶחָד חָכָם, וְאֶחָד רָשָׁע, וְאֶחָד תָּם, וְאֶחָד שֶׁאֵינוֹ יוֹדֵעַ לִשְׁאוֹל:

חָכָם מָה הוּא אוֹמֵר? מָה הָעֵדֹת וְהַחֻקִּים וְהַמִּשְׁפָּטִים, אֲשֶׁר צִוָּה יְיָ אֱלֹהֵינוּ אֶתְכֶם? וְאַף אַתָּה אֱמָר־לוֹ כְּהִלְכוֹת הַפֶּסַח: אֵין מַפְטִירִין אַחַר הַפֶּסַח אֲפִיקוֹמָן:

רָשָׁע מָה הוּא אוֹמֵר? מָה הָעֲבֹדָה הַזֹּאת לָכֶם? לָכֶם וְלֹא לוֹ. וּלְפִי שֶׁהוֹצִיא אֶת־עַצְמוֹ מִן הַכְּלָל, כָּפַר בָּעִקָּר. וְאַף אַתָּה הַקְהֵה אֶת־שִׁנָּיו, וֶאֱמָר־לוֹ: בַּעֲבוּר זֶה, עָשָׂה יְיָ לִי, בְּצֵאתִי מִמִּצְרַיִם, לִי וְלֹא־לוֹ. אִלּוּ הָיָה שָׁם, לֹא הָיָה נִגְאָל:

תָּם מָה הוּא אוֹמֵר? מַה זֹּאת? וְאָמַרְתָּ אֵלָיו: בְּחֹזֶק יָד הוֹצִיאָנוּ יְיָ מִמִּצְרַיִם מִבֵּית עֲבָדִים:

וְשֶׁאֵינוֹ יוֹדֵעַ לִשְׁאוֹל, אַתְּ פְּתַח לוֹ. שֶׁנֶּאֱמַר: וְהִגַּדְתָּ לְבִנְךָ, בַּיּוֹם הַהוּא לֵאמֹר: בַּעֲבוּר זֶה עָשָׂה יְיָ לִי, בְּצֵאתִי מִמִּצְרָיִם:

יָכוֹל מֵרֹאשׁ חֹדֶשׁ, תַּלְמוּד לוֹמַר בַּיּוֹם הַהוּא. אִי בַּיּוֹם הַהוּא. יָכוֹל מִבְּעוֹד יוֹם. תַּלְמוּד לוֹמַר. בַּעֲבוּר זֶה. בַּעֲבוּר זֶה לֹא אָמַרְתִּי, אֶלָּא בְּשָׁעָה שֶׁיֵּשׁ מַצָּה וּמָרוֹר מֻנָּחִים לְפָנֶיךָ:

Do you think the Four Children are the same age or are different ages? How do you picture each one?

There is a little of the four children in each of us. Describe situations where you felt wise, rebellious, simple, or not even able to ask a question. How did this affect how you learned?

The rabbis wanted to teach the story of the Exodus to all children. How do you feel, though, about the answers they gave to each of the Four Children? Would you make any changes?

The Four Children make an "appearance" at our Seder and we have the opportunity to answer their questions. How can we bring the apathetic or disengaged child (or adult) to the Seder table?

The Story of Passover

Our story begins with the patriarchs and matriarchs of old—Abraham and Sarah, Isaac and Rebecca, Jacob, Leah and Rachel. God made a covenant with them, promising that their descendants would be as numerous as the stars and that they would become a great nation. But first, their descendants would sojourn in a foreign land for four hundred years where they would be enslaved and finally set free. Then, God said, the Israelites would return to the land of their ancestors.

The sojourn to Egypt came about because the jealous brothers of Joseph, the favorite son of the patriarch Jacob, sold him into slavery. Joseph was taken to Egypt. Eventually, he became an advisor to the Pharaoh because of his ability to interpret

[Traditional Text]

מִתְּחִלָּה עוֹבְדֵי עֲבוֹדָה זָרָה הָיוּ אֲבוֹתֵינוּ. וְעַכְשָׁו קֵרְבָנוּ הַמָּקוֹם לַעֲבוֹדָתוֹ. שֶׁנֶּאֱמַר: וַיֹּאמֶר יְהוֹשֻׁעַ אֶל־כָּל־הָעָם. כֹּה אָמַר יְיָ אֱלֹהֵי יִשְׂרָאֵל, בְּעֵבֶר הַנָּהָר יָשְׁבוּ אֲבוֹתֵיכֶם מֵעוֹלָם, תֶּרַח אֲבִי אַבְרָהָם וַאֲבִי נָחוֹר. וַיַּעַבְדוּ אֱלֹהִים אֲחֵרִים: וָאֶקַּח אֶת־אֲבִיכֶם אֶת־אַבְרָהָם מֵעֵבֶר הַנָּהָר, וָאוֹלֵךְ אוֹתוֹ בְּכָל־אֶרֶץ כְּנָעַן. וָאַרְבֶּה אֶת־זַרְעוֹ, וָאֶתֶּן לוֹ אֶת־יִצְחָק: וָאֶתֵּן לְיִצְחָק אֶת־יַעֲקֹב וְאֶת־עֵשָׂו. וָאֶתֵּן לְעֵשָׂו אֶת־הַר שֵׂעִיר, לָרֶשֶׁת אוֹתוֹ. וְיַעֲקֹב וּבָנָיו יָרְדוּ מִצְרָיִם:

בָּרוּךְ שׁוֹמֵר הַבְטָחָתוֹ לְיִשְׂרָאֵל. בָּרוּךְ הוּא. שֶׁהַקָּדוֹשׁ בָּרוּךְ הוּא חִשַּׁב אֶת־הַקֵּץ, לַעֲשׂוֹת כְּמָה שֶׁאָמַר לְאַבְרָהָם אָבִינוּ בִּבְרִית בֵּין הַבְּתָרִים, שֶׁנֶּאֱמַר: וַיֹּאמֶר לְאַבְרָם יָדֹעַ תֵּדַע, כִּי־גֵר יִהְיֶה זַרְעֲךָ, בְּאֶרֶץ לֹא לָהֶם, וַעֲבָדוּם וְעִנּוּ אֹתָם אַרְבַּע מֵאוֹת שָׁנָה: וְגַם אֶת־הַגּוֹי אֲשֶׁר יַעֲבֹדוּ דָּן

dreams. Joseph instructed Pharaoh to build storehouses for grain to feed the people during seven years of famine that would follow seven years of plenty.

When famine came as predicted, Joseph's brothers traveled to Egypt to purchase food. Joseph revealed himself to them and invited his whole family to settle there. Here in Egypt, Jacob's household multiplied and lived peacefully for many years, until a new Pharaoh arose "who knew not Joseph" and did not remember his wise counsel. This Pharaoh feared that the Hebrews would become too numerous and join his enemies to fight against him.

The new Pharaoh decided to make the Hebrews slaves, forcing them to do harsh labor. They were assigned to build garrison cities with bricks made from clay and straw. However, the more the Hebrews were oppressed, the more they increased. Pharaoh then decreed that all male babies

אָנֹכִי. וְאַחֲרֵי כֵן יֵצְאוּ, בִּרְכֻשׁ גָּדוֹל:

(מכסים את המצות ומגביהים את הכוס)
וְהִיא שֶׁעָמְדָה לַאֲבוֹתֵינוּ וְלָנוּ. שֶׁלֹּא אֶחָד בִּלְבָד, עָמַד עָלֵינוּ לְכַלּוֹתֵנוּ. אֶלָּא שֶׁבְּכָל
בָּרוּךְ הוּא מַצִּילֵנוּ מִיָּדָם:

צֵא וּלְמַד, מַה בִּקֵּשׁ לָבָן הָאֲרַמִּי לַעֲשׂוֹת לְיַעֲקֹב אָבִינוּ. שֶׁפַּרְעֹה לֹא גָזַר אֶלָּא עַל הַזְּכָרִים, וְלָבָן בִּקֵּשׁ לַעֲקֹר אֶת־הַכֹּל, שֶׁנֶּאֱמַר: אֲרַמִּי אֹבֵד אָבִי, וַיֵּרֶד מִצְרַיְמָה, וַיָּגָר שָׁם בִּמְתֵי מְעָט.וַיְהִי שָׁם לְגוֹי גָּדוֹל, עָצוּם וָרָב:

וַיֵּרֶד מִצְרַיְמָה, אָנוּס עַל פִּי הַדִּבּוּר. וַיָּגָר שָׁם. מְלַמֵּד שֶׁלֹּא יָרַד יַעֲקֹב אָבִינוּ לְהִשְׁתַּקֵּעַ בְּמִצְרַיִם, אֶלָּא לָגוּר שָׁם, שֶׁנֶּאֱמַר: וַיֹּאמְרוּ אֶל־פַּרְעֹה, לָגוּר בָּאָרֶץ בָּאנוּ, כִּי אֵין מִרְעֶה לַצֹּאן אֲשֶׁר לַעֲבָדֶיךָ, כִּי כָבֵד הָרָעָב בְּאֶרֶץ כְּנָעַן. וְעַתָּה, יֵשְׁבוּ־נָא עֲבָדֶיךָ בְּאֶרֶץ גֹּשֶׁן:

בִּמְתֵי מְעָט. כְּמָה שֶׁנֶּאֱמַר: בְּשִׁבְעִים נֶפֶשׁ,

THE ROSENSTEIN HAGGADAH

be killed. The midwives, Shifra and Puah, fearing God, defied Pharaoh and let them live. Their clever ruse was to report that the Hebrew women were too vigorous and gave birth before they arrived. Seeing his evil plan thwarted, Pharaoh then decreed "Every boy that is born, you shall throw him into the Nile."

One Hebrew mother, Yocheved, feared she could no longer hide her baby. She made the heart-rending decision to place the baby in a basket to float on the river. The child's older sister Miriam hid in the reeds to watch. She observed the Pharaoh's daughter bathing in the Nile. When the princess heard the infant crying, she took pity on him. Defying her father's cruel decree, she rescued the helpless baby. She named him Moshe (Moses) meaning drawn from the water and adopted him as her own. Miriam bravely stepped forward, offering to find a nurse for the child. When Pharaoh's daughter agreed, she ran to fetch Yocheved. Although Moses was raised in the royal palace, the Torah tells us nothing of his childhood. The story continues with Moses as a man.

Once, when Moses saw an Egyptian taskmaster beating a Hebrew slave, he could not control his anger and killed him. When he learned that his action was known, he feared for his life and fled to the land of Midian. Here he saved the seven daughters of the Midianite priest Jethro from some rowdy shepherds. His good deed brought him to dwell in Jethro's household and marry Tzipporah, one of his daughters, with whom he had two sons. Moses became a shepherd and tended his father-in-law's flock.

There is a legend that once, when Moses

יָרְדוּ אֲבֹתֶיךָ מִצְרָיְמָה. וְעַתָּה, שָׂמְךָ יְיָ אֱלֹהֶיךָ, כְּכוֹכְבֵי הַשָּׁמַיִם לָרֹב.

וַיְהִי שָׁם לְגוֹי. מְלַמֵּד שֶׁהָיוּ יִשְׂרָאֵל מְצֻיָּנִים שָׁם:

גָּדוֹל עָצוּם, כְּמָה שֶׁנֶּאֱמַר: וּבְנֵי יִשְׂרָאֵל, פָּרוּ וַיִּשְׁרְצוּ, וַיִּרְבּוּ וַיַּעַצְמוּ, בִּמְאֹד מְאֹד, וַתִּמָּלֵא הָאָרֶץ אֹתָם:

וָרָב. כְּמָה שֶׁנֶּאֱמַר: רְבָבָה כְּצֶמַח הַשָּׂדֶה נְתַתִּיךְ, וַתִּרְבִּי, וַתִּגְדְּלִי, וַתָּבֹאִי בַּעֲדִי עֲדָיִים: שָׁדַיִם נָכֹנוּ, וּשְׂעָרֵךְ צִמֵּחַ, וְאַתְּ עֵרֹם וְעֶרְיָה:

וָאֶעֱבֹר עָלַיִךְ וָאֶרְאֵךְ מִתְבּוֹסֶסֶת בְּדָמָיִךְ וָאֹמַר לָךְ בְּדָמַיִךְ חֲיִי וָאֹמַר לָךְ בְּדָמַיִךְ חֲיִי.

וַיָּרֵעוּ אֹתָנוּ הַמִּצְרִים וַיְעַנּוּנוּ. וַיִּתְּנוּ עָלֵינוּ עֲבֹדָה קָשָׁה. וַיָּרֵעוּ אֹתָנוּ הַמִּצְרִים. כְּמָה שֶׁנֶּאֱמַר: הָבָה נִתְחַכְּמָה לוֹ. פֶּן יִרְבֶּה, וְהָיָה כִּי תִקְרֶאנָה מִלְחָמָה, וְנוֹסַף גַּם הוּא עַל שֹׂנְאֵינוּ, וְנִלְחַם־בָּנוּ וְעָלָה מִן הָאָרֶץ:

וַיְעַנּוּנוּ. כְּמָה שֶׁנֶּאֱמַר: וַיָּשִׂימוּ עָלָיו שָׂרֵי מִסִּים, לְמַעַן עַנֹּתוֹ בְּסִבְלֹתָם: וַיִּבֶן עָרֵי מִסְכְּנוֹת לְפַרְעֹה, אֶת־פִּתֹם וְאֶת־רַעַמְסֵס: וַיִּתְּנוּ עָלֵינוּ עֲבֹדָה קָשָׁה. כְּמָה שֶׁנֶּאֱמַר: וַיַּעֲבִדוּ מִצְרַיִם אֶת־בְּנֵי יִשְׂרָאֵל בְּפָרֶךְ:

וַנִּצְעַק אֶל־יְיָ אֱלֹהֵי אֲבֹתֵינוּ, וַיִּשְׁמַע יְיָ אֶת־ קֹלֵנוּ, וַיַּרְא אֶת־עָנְיֵנוּ, וְאֶת־עֲמָלֵנוּ, וְאֶת לַחֲצֵנוּ: וַנִּצְעַק אֶל־יְיָ אֱלֹהֵי אֲבֹתֵינוּ, כְּמָה שֶׁנֶּאֱמַר: וַיְהִי בַיָּמִים הָרַבִּים הָהֵם, וַיָּמָת מֶלֶךְ מִצְרַיִם, וַיֵּאָנְחוּ בְנֵי־יִשְׂרָאֵל מִן־הָעֲבֹדָה וַיִּזְעָקוּ. וַתַּעַל שַׁוְעָתָם אֶל־הָאֱלֹהִים מִן־ הָעֲבֹדָה:

וַיִּשְׁמַע יְיָ אֶת־קֹלֵנוּ. כְּמָה שֶׁנֶּאֱמַר: וַיִּשְׁמַע אֱלֹהִים אֶת־נַאֲקָתָם, וַיִּזְכֹּר אֱלֹהִים אֶת־ בְּרִיתוֹ, אֶת־אַבְרָהָם, אֶת־יִצְחָק, וְאֶת יַעֲקֹב:

וַיַּרְא אֶת־עָנְיֵנוּ: זוֹ פְּרִישׁוּת דֶּרֶךְ אֶרֶץ. כְּמָה שֶׁנֶּאֱמַר: וַיַּרְא אֱלֹהִים אֶת־בְּנֵי יִשְׂרָאֵל. וַיֵּדַע אֱלֹהִים:

was tending the sheep, a little lamb strayed from the flock. Though tired from the long day, Moses searched until he found the lamb and tenderly carried it back to the flock. God saw this loving act and decided that someone who cared so much for this little lamb would surely take good care of the "flock of Israel."

While tending sheep on Mount Horeb, God appeared to Moses in a burning bush that was not consumed. From the bush, God's voice called to him saying, "I am the God of your ancestors. I have seen the suffering of the people Israel and have heard their cries. I am ready to take them out of Egypt and bring them to a new land, one that is flowing with milk and honey."

God then told Moses to return to Egypt to bring the message of freedom to the Hebrews and to warn Pharaoh to let the slaves go or suffer terrible consequences. The humble Moses tried five times to refuse, believing that the Hebrews would not accept him as God's messenger, nor would Pharaoh listen to him.

"I will be with you" God promised, and gave Moses the words to convince the Hebrews that he was God's messenger and the signs to demonstrate God's power to Pharaoh. God also assured Moses, who described himself as being "slow of speech and slow of tongue", that his older brother Aaron could be his "mouthpiece." With these assurances, Moses said farewell to Jethro, who told him to go in peace. Then he set out for Egypt.

With Aaron by his side, Moses became the leader of the Hebrews. He returned to his childhood home to confront the Pharaoh. The signs and wonders Moses performed

וְאֶת־עֲמָלֵנוּ. אֵלוּ הַבָּנִים. כְּמָה שֶׁנֶּאֱמַר: כָּל־הַבֵּן הַיִּלּוֹד הַיְאֹרָה תַּשְׁלִיכֻהוּ, וְכָל־הַבַּת תְּחַיּוּן:

וְאֶת־לַחֲצֵנוּ. זֶה הַדְּחַק. כְּמָה שֶׁנֶּאֱמַר: וְגַם־רָאִיתִי אֶת־הַלַּחַץ, אֲשֶׁר מִצְרַיִם לֹחֲצִים אֹתָם:

וַיּוֹצִאֵנוּ יְיָ מִמִּצְרַיִם, בְּיָד חֲזָקָה, וּבִזְרֹעַ נְטוּיָה, וּבְמֹרָא גָּדֹל וּבְאֹתוֹת וּבְמֹפְתִים:

וַיּוֹצִאֵנוּ יְיָ מִמִּצְרַיִם. לֹא עַל־יְדֵי מַלְאָךְ, וְלֹא עַל־יְדֵי שָׂרָף, וְלֹא עַל־יְדֵי שָׁלִיחַ. אֶלָּא הַקָּדוֹשׁ בָּרוּךְ הוּא בִּכְבוֹדוֹ וּבְעַצְמוֹ. שֶׁנֶּאֱמַר: וְעָבַרְתִּי בְאֶרֶץ מִצְרַיִם בַּלַּיְלָה הַזֶּה, וְהִכֵּיתִי כָל־בְּכוֹר בְּאֶרֶץ מִצְרַיִם, מֵאָדָם וְעַד בְּהֵמָה, וּבְכָל־אֱלֹהֵי מִצְרַיִם אֶעֱשֶׂה שְׁפָטִים אֲנִי יְיָ:

וְעָבַרְתִּי בְאֶרֶץ־מִצְרַיִם בַּלַּיְלָה הַזֶּה, אֲנִי וְלֹא מַלְאָךְ. וְהִכֵּיתִי כָל בְּכוֹר בְּאֶרֶץ־מִצְרַיִם. אֲנִי וְלֹא שָׂרָף. וּבְכָל־אֱלֹהֵי מִצְרַיִם אֶעֱשֶׂה שְׁפָטִים, אֲנִי וְלֹא הַשָּׁלִיחַ. אֲנִי יְיָ, אֲנִי הוּא וְלֹא אַחֵר:

בְּיָד חֲזָקָה. זוֹ הַדֶּבֶר. כְּמָה שֶׁנֶּאֱמַר: הִנֵּה יַד־יְיָ הוֹיָה, בְּמִקְנְךָ אֲשֶׁר בַּשָּׂדֶה, בַּסּוּסִים בַּחֲמֹרִים בַּגְּמַלִּים, בַּבָּקָר וּבַצֹּאן, דֶּבֶר כָּבֵד מְאֹד:

וּבִזְרֹעַ נְטוּיָה. זוֹ הַחֶרֶב. כְּמָה שֶׁנֶּאֱמַר: וְחַרְבּוֹ שְׁלוּפָה בְּיָדוֹ, נְטוּיָה עַל־יְרוּשָׁלָיִם:

וּבְמֹרָא גָּדֹל, זֶה גִּלּוּי שְׁכִינָה. כְּמָה שֶׁנֶּאֱמַר: אוֹ הֲנִסָּה אֱלֹהִים, לָבוֹא לָקַחַת לוֹ גוֹי מִקֶּרֶב גּוֹי, בְּמַסֹּת בְּאֹתֹת וּבְמוֹפְתִים וּבְמִלְחָמָה, וּבְיָד חֲזָקָה וּבִזְרוֹעַ נְטוּיָה, וּבְמוֹרָאִים גְּדֹלִים. כְּכֹל אֲשֶׁר־עָשָׂה לָכֶם יְיָ אֱלֹהֵיכֶם בְּמִצְרַיִם, לְעֵינֶיךָ:

וּבְאֹתוֹת, זֶה הַמַּטֶּה, כְּמָה שֶׁנֶּאֱמַר: וְאֶת הַמַּטֶּה הַזֶּה תִּקַּח בְּיָדְךָ. אֲשֶׁר תַּעֲשֶׂה־בּוֹ אֶת־הָאֹתֹת:

וּבְמֹפְתִים. זֶה הַדָּם. כְּמָה שֶׁנֶּאֱמַר: וְנָתַתִּי

THE ROSENSTEIN HAGGADAH

did not impress Pharaoh and he refused to comply. He forced the Hebrews to work even harder, making their own straw for the bricks they needed for building. God, as promised, brought ten plagues on the Egyptians. Even the suffering of his own people did not move Pharaoh. Although frightened, Pharaoh was stubborn. He said he would let the Hebrews go, but kept changing his mind. Pharaoh did not relent until the final plague, the slaying of the first born in all of Egypt, included his own household. This convinced Pharaoh to let them go!

מוֹפְתִים, בַּשָּׁמַיִם וּבָאָרֶץ

(נוהגים להטיף מעט מן הכוס בעת אמירת דם ואש, וגם באמירת דם צפרדע, וכו׳, וגם באמירת דצ״ך עד״ש וכו׳)

דָּם. וָאֵשׁ. וְתִימְרוֹת עָשָׁן:

דָּבָר אַחֵר. בְּיָד חֲזָקָה שְׁתַּיִם. וּבִזְרֹעַ נְטוּיָה שְׁתַּיִם. וּבְמוֹרָא גָּדוֹל שְׁתַּיִם. וּבְאֹתוֹת שְׁתַּיִם. וּבְמֹפְתִים שְׁתַּיִם: אֵלּוּ עֶשֶׂר מַכּוֹת שֶׁהֵבִיא הַקָּדוֹשׁ בָּרוּךְ הוּא עַל־הַמִּצְרִים בְּמִצְרַיִם, וְאֵלּוּ הֵן:

The Ten Plagues

We now fill our wine cups to remember our great joy in being able to leave Egypt, yet our happiness is diminished because the Egyptians, who are also God's children, suffered because of Pharaoh's hardness of heart and cruel leadership. Therefore, we spill a drop of wine from our own cups (with a finger or a spoon) as we recite each plague.

Blood	*Dam*	דָם
Frogs	*Tz'fardaiya*	צְפַרְדֵעַ
Lice	*Kinim*	כִּנִים
Beasts	*Arov*	עָרוֹב
Cattle Disease	*Dever*	דֶבֶר
Boils	*Sh'chin*	שְׁחִין
Hail	*Barad*	בָּרָד
Locusts	*Arbeh*	אַרְבֶּה
Darkness	*Choshech*	חֹשֶׁךְ
Plague of the Firstborn	*Makat B'chorot*	מַכַּת בְּכוֹרוֹת

THE ROSENSTEIN HAGGADAH

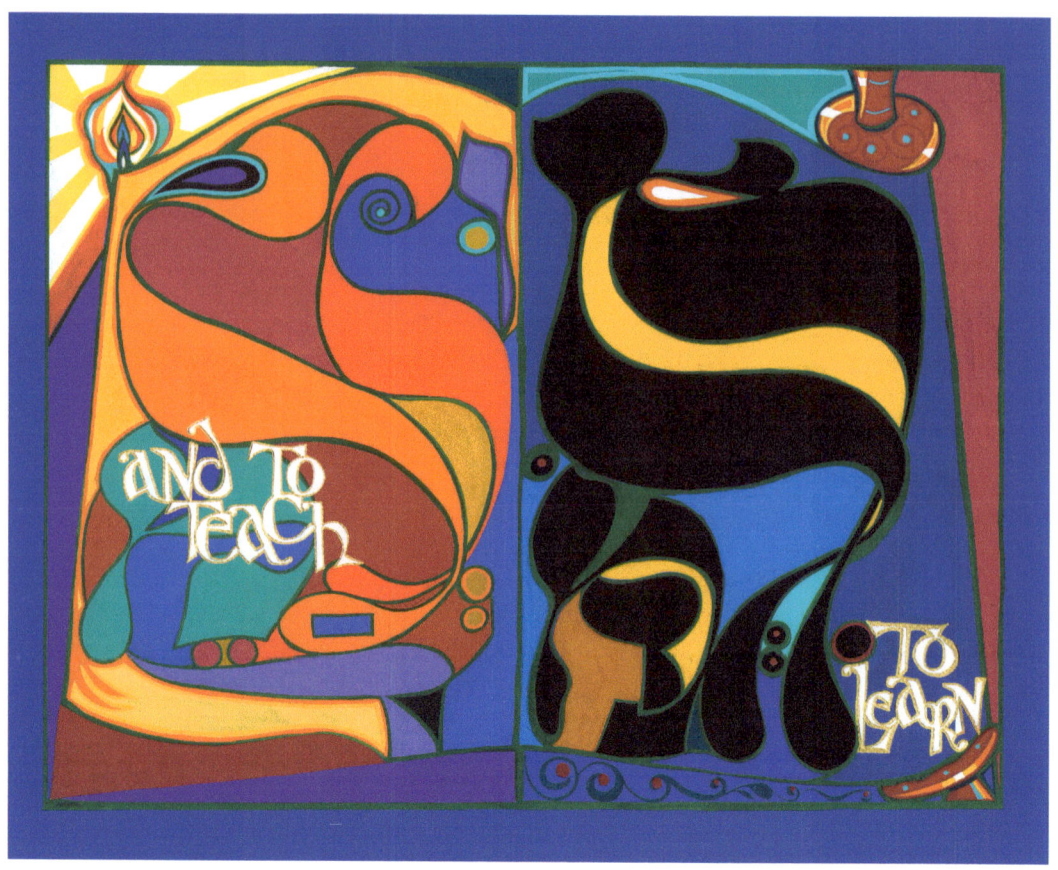

[Traditional Text]

רַבִּי יְהוּדָה הָיָה נוֹתֵן בָּהֶם סִמָּנִים: דְּצַ"ךְ עֲדַ"שׁ בְּאַחַ"ב:

רַבִּי יוֹסֵי הַגְּלִילִי אוֹמֵר: מִנַּיִן אַתָּה אוֹמֵר, שֶׁלָּקוּ הַמִּצְרִיִּים בְּמִצְרַיִם עֶשֶׂר מַכּוֹת, וְעַל הַיָּם, לָקוּ חֲמִשִּׁים מַכּוֹת? בְּמִצְרַיִם מָה הוּא אוֹמֵר: וַיֹּאמְרוּ הַחַרְטֻמִּם אֶל-פַּרְעֹה, אֶצְבַּע אֱלֹהִים הִוא. וְעַל הַיָּם מָה הוּא אוֹמֵר? וַיַּרְא יִשְׂרָאֵל אֶת-הַיָּד הַגְּדֹלָה, אֲשֶׁר עָשָׂה יְיָ בְּמִצְרַיִם, וַיִּירְאוּ הָעָם אֶת-יְיָ, וַיַּאֲמִינוּ בַּיְיָ, וּבְמֹשֶׁה עַבְדּוֹ. כַּמָּה לָקוּ בְּאֶצְבַּע, עֶשֶׂר מַכּוֹת: אֱמוֹר מֵעַתָּה, בְּמִצְרַיִם לָקוּ עֶשֶׂר מַכּוֹת, וְעַל-הַיָּם, לָקוּ חֲמִשִּׁים מַכּוֹת:

רַבִּי אֱלִיעֶזֶר אוֹמֵר: מִנַּיִן שֶׁכָּל-מַכָּה וּמַכָּה, שֶׁהֵבִיא הַקָּדוֹשׁ בָּרוּךְ הוּא עַל הַמִּצְרִיִּים בְּמִצְרַיִם, הָיְתָה שֶׁל אַרְבַּע מַכּוֹת? שֶׁנֶּאֱמַר: יְשַׁלַּח-בָּם חֲרוֹן אַפּוֹ, עֶבְרָה וָזַעַם וְצָרָה, מִשְׁלַחַת מַלְאֲכֵי רָעִים. עֶבְרָה אַחַת. וָזַעַם שְׁתַּיִם. וְצָרָה שָׁלֹשׁ. מִשְׁלַחַת מַלְאֲכֵי רָעִים אַרְבַּע: אֱמוֹר מֵעַתָּה, בְּמִצְרַיִם לָקוּ אַרְבָּעִים מַכּוֹת, וְעַל הַיָּם לָקוּ מָאתַיִם מַכּוֹת:

רַבִּי עֲקִיבָא אוֹמֵר: מִנַּיִן שֶׁכָּל-מַכָּה וּמַכָּה, שֶׁהֵבִיא הַקָּדוֹשׁ בָּרוּךְ הוּא עַל הַמִּצְרִיִּים בְּמִצְרַיִם, הָיְתָה שֶׁל חָמֵשׁ מַכּוֹת? שֶׁנֶּאֱמַר: יְשַׁלַּח-בָּם חֲרוֹן אַפּוֹ, עֶבְרָה וָזַעַם וְצָרָה, מִשְׁלַחַת מַלְאֲכֵי רָעִים. חֲרוֹן אַפּוֹ אַחַת. עֶבְרָה שְׁתַּיִם. וָזַעַם שָׁלֹשׁ. וְצָרָה אַרְבַּע. מִשְׁלַחַת מַלְאֲכֵי רָעִים חָמֵשׁ: אֱמוֹר מֵעַתָּה, בְּמִצְרַיִם לָקוּ חֲמִשִּׁים מַכּוֹת, וְעַל הַיָּם לָקוּ חֲמִשִּׁים וּמָאתַיִם מַכּוֹת:

THE ROSENSTEIN HAGGADAH

CROSSING THE SEA TO FREEDOM

Soon after Pharaoh allowed the Hebrews to leave, he regretted his decision and changed his mind, ordering his army to bring them back to Egypt. As the people of Israel reached the Sea of Reeds, they saw the Egyptians approaching and were filled with terror. God told Moses to lift his rod and when he did, a strong east wind drove back the sea, leaving space for the Hebrews to cross over on dry land. The Egyptians pursued them, but Moses again lifted his rod and the waters rushed back, drowning the soldiers.

Then Miriam, the sister of Moses and Aaron, took her timbrel in her hand, and all the women followed her in a glorious dance of victory. She led them chanting, "Sing to God who has triumphed gloriously. Horse and rider are hurled into the sea." (Exodus 15:20-21)

Thus God brought us out of Egypt, not by an angel, not by a seraph, and not by a messenger, but alone, with a mighty hand and an outstretched arm, with great terror and with signs and wonders.

THE ROSENSTEIN HAGGADAH

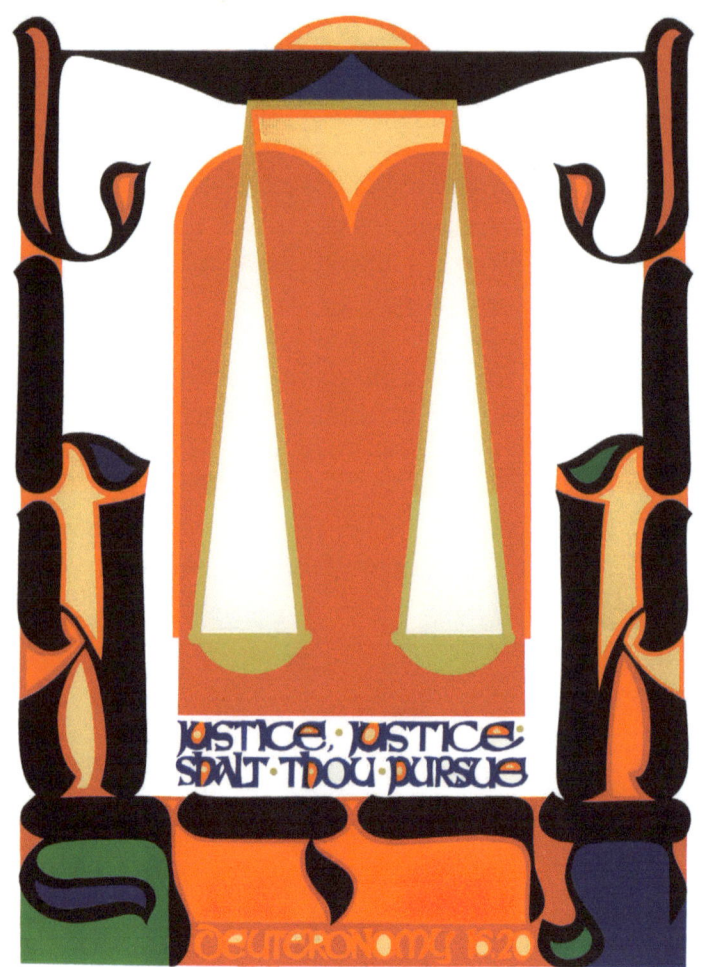

A Maggid Seder Song

Let My People Go

(The Biblical story of the Exodus has inspired many people in many places to seek freedom. *Let My People Go* is an African-American spiritual.)

Verse 1 When Israel was in Egypt land - let my people go. Oppressed so hard they could not stand. Let my people Go.

Chorus: Go down Moses, way down in Egypt land. Tell ol' Pharaoh to let my people go.

Verse 2 Thus saith the Lord bold Moses said. Let my people go. If not I'll smite your first born dead. Let my people go.

Chorus

"GET WISDOM, GAIN UNDERSTANDING" PROVERBS 4:5

Maggid Commentaries and Questions for Discussion

In Hebrew the word *Mitzrayim*, means a narrow place. Being in *Mitzrayim* can be both a physical or spiritual condition. What makes you stuck in a rut? What helps you leave your *Mitzrayim*?

Some scholars say there is no demonstrable historic basis for a Hebrew presence in the land of Egypt. Therefore, the Exodus story is a myth. Others disagree. Does it make a difference to you if the story was historical or mythical?

There is no evidence that the Hebrews would have turned against the Pharaoh, yet his irrational fear turns him against them. When have you seen this kind of behavior occur?

Pharaoh distanced himself emotionally and psychologically from the evil he decreed. For example, he assigned midwives the task of murdering newborns, and his soldiers the task of throwing baby boys into the sea. How have modern tyrants designed evil plans for others to enact?

The Torah verse, "And the Egyptians made the Israelites serve with vigor" indicates that ordinary Egyptians were involved in the oppression and were immune to the suffering of the Israelite people. They shared in the guilt and thus were punished.

How can we apply pressure for change? Can there be liberation without violence?

The midwives, Shifra and Puah, performed the first recorded act of civil disobedience. Have you ever been involved with civil disobedience? Share your experience.

Why do you think the Torah tells us the names of the midwives, but omits the name of the Pharaoh? (Most historians believe he was Ramses II.)

The Midrash refers to Pharaoh's daughter as "Batya", meaning daughter of God. This teaches us that the righteous of all peoples have merit.

In the Torah text, when Moses seeks to know God's name, God replies, "I Will Be What I Will Be." How would you interpret this name?

What kind of leadership do you think we need now in our country, in Israel, and the world?

What is the purpose of the Ten Plagues?
- To punish the Egyptians
- To display God's might to both the Egyptians and the Israelites
- To add drama to the story

We note in the plagues that direct violence against human beings is used as a last resort to achieve political results. How does this apply to our world today?

Before the final plague, the Hebrews were instructed to mark their doorposts with the blood of lambs, so the angel of death would "pass over" their homes, hence the name of the holiday.

The rabbis taught that those Hebrews who refused to leave Egypt were not just foolish, but wicked. For a Jew to be free is not an opportunity, it is considered an obligation. Do you agree or disagree? Why do some not find freedom an imperative?

There is a legend that the sea did not split until one person, Nachson ben Aminadav, had the courage to step in. When were you the first to "step in" like Nachson and when did you stay on the sidelines?

The Torah says nothing about Miriam's personal life. What do you imagine? Could she have had a "career" as a prophet, as well as been a wife and mother?

There is an old Jewish saying, "Pray as if everything depended on God, and act as if everything depended on you." How does this saying relate to the Passover story?

Since the Ethiopians identified so strongly with the story of the Exodus, the famous airlift that brought them to Israel was called Operation Moses.

God's Promise

(The matzot are covered and the wine lifted.)

וְהִיא שֶׁעָמְדָה לַאֲבוֹתֵינוּ וְלָנוּ. שֶׁלֹּא אֶחָד בִּלְבָד, עָמַד עָלֵינוּ לְכַלוֹתֵנוּ. אֶלָּא שֶׁבְּכָל דּוֹר וָדוֹר, עוֹמְדִים עָלֵינוּ לְכַלוֹתֵנוּ. וְהַקָּדוֹשׁ בָּרוּךְ הוּא מַצִילֵנוּ מִיָּדָם:

Vehi she'amdah la'avoteinu v'lanu. Shelo echad bilvad, amad aleinu l'chaloteinu. Ela sheb'chol dor vador, omdim aleinu l'chaloteinu. VeHakadosh, Baruch Hu, matzileinu miyadam.

It is the promise of redemption that has sustained the Jewish people in each generation, as enemies arose who sought to destroy us. And the Holy One of Blessing saved us from their hand.

Dayenu
(It Would Have Been Sufficient)

How grateful we are for all the different acts of kindness that Adonai has done for us!

Ilu hotzianu miMitzraim . . . . *Dayenu*

Ilu natan lanu et haShabbat . . . . *Dayenu*

Ilu natan lanu et haTorah . . . . *Dayenu*

God. . .

Took us out of Egypt . . . . Dayenu

Punished the Egyptians and
destroyed their idols . . . . Dayenu

Divided the Sea of Reeds and
led us across on dry land . . . . Dayenu

Took care of us in the desert
and fed us manna . . . . Dayenu

Gave us Shabbat . . . . Dayenu

Brought us to Mount Sinai and
gave us the Torah . . . . Dayenu

Brought us to Israel and built
the Temple . . . . Dayenu

For all these, we say . . . . Dayenu

כַּמָה מַעֲלוֹת טוֹבוֹת לַמָּקוֹם עָלֵינוּ:

אִלּוּ הוֹצִיאָנוּ מִמִּצְרַיִם,
וְלֹא עָשָׂה בָהֶם שְׁפָטִים, דַּיֵּנוּ:

אִלּוּ עָשָׂה בָהֶם שְׁפָטִים,
וְלֹא עָשָׂה בֵאלֹהֵיהֶם, דַּיֵּנוּ:

אִלּוּ עָשָׂה בֵאלֹהֵיהֶם,
וְלֹא הָרַג אֶת־בְּכוֹרֵיהֶם, דַּיֵּנוּ:

אִלּוּ הָרַג אֶת־בְּכוֹרֵיהֶם,
וְלֹא נָתַן לָנוּ אֶת־מָמוֹנָם, דַּיֵּנוּ:

אִלּוּ נָתַן לָנוּ אֶת־מָמוֹנָם,
וְלֹא קָרַע לָנוּ אֶת־הַיָּם, דַּיֵּנוּ:

אִלּוּ קָרַע לָנוּ אֶת־הַיָּם,
וְלֹא הֶעֱבִירָנוּ בְתוֹכוֹ בֶּחָרָבָה, דַּיֵּנוּ:

אִלּוּ הֶעֱבִירָנוּ בְתוֹכוֹ בֶּחָרָבָה,
וְלֹא שִׁקַּע צָרֵינוּ בְּתוֹכוֹ, דַּיֵּנוּ:

אִלּוּ שִׁקַּע צָרֵינוּ בְּתוֹכוֹ,
וְלֹא סִפֵּק צָרְכֵּנוּ בַּמִּדְבָּר אַרְבָּעִים שָׁנָה, דַּיֵּנוּ:

אִלּוּ סִפֵּק צָרְכֵּנוּ בַּמִּדְבָּר אַרְבָּעִים שָׁנָה,
וְלֹא הֶאֱכִילָנוּ אֶת־הַמָּן, דַּיֵּנוּ:

אִלּוּ הֶאֱכִילָנוּ אֶת־הַמָּן,
וְלֹא נָתַן לָנוּ אֶת־הַשַּׁבָּת, דַּיֵּנוּ:

אִלּוּ נָתַן לָנוּ אֶת־הַשַּׁבָּת,
וְלֹא קֵרְבָנוּ לִפְנֵי הַר סִינַי, דַּיֵּנוּ:

אִלּוּ קֵרְבָנוּ לִפְנֵי הַר סִינַי,
וְלֹא נָתַן לָנוּ אֶת־הַתּוֹרָה, דַּיֵּנוּ:

אִלּוּ נָתַן לָנוּ אֶת־הַתּוֹרָה,
וְלֹא הִכְנִיסָנוּ לְאֶרֶץ יִשְׂרָאֵל, דַּיֵּנוּ:

אִלּוּ הִכְנִיסָנוּ לְאֶרֶץ יִשְׂרָאֵל,
וְלֹא בָנָה לָנוּ אֶת־בֵּית הַבְּחִירָה, דַּיֵּנוּ:

It is an Iranian custom to "whip" each other with a scallion during the singing of Dayenu to recall the beatings the slaves endured.[27]

Obviously, God was not satisfied until all the steps to our deliverance were achieved.

The Passover Symbols

Raban Gamliel would say, "Those who have not explained three things during the Seder have not fulfilled their obligation. These three things are: Pesach, Matzah, and Maror."

Pesach
Our ancestors ate a Passover offering at the time the Temple stood to remember that God passed over the houses of the Hebrews during the tenth plague.

Matzah
The matzah reminds us that our ancestors left Egypt in such great haste that the dough for their bread did not have time to rise.

Maror
Maror reminds us of how bitter the Egyptians made the lives of our ancestors when they were slaves.

Pesach (paschal lamb)

The Hebrews risked their lives slaughtering an animal for the Passover offering that was holy to the Egyptians. In this way, they distanced themselves from paganism and idolatry. From what do we need to distance ourselves today?

The Hebrew ate the paschal lamb with their loins girded, their shoes on, with staff in hand, ready to leave. How can we prepare to face our own challenges?

The sacrifice of the lamb on Passover was permitted until the destruction of the Temple. Since then, Ashkenazim have been forbidden to eat lamb meat on Passover, but it is the featured dish at the Seder meal for some Sephardim.

Matzah

Matzah is called both the bread of poverty and the bread of freedom. How can you explain this?

Just as our ancestors left for freedom in great haste, so we too must move quickly to work for freedom and redemption.

Maror

Ashkenazim usually use horseradish for maror; Sephardim and Mizrachim (Eastern) Jews use romaine lettuce, escarole or endive lettuce.

Why do you think we recite a blessing upon eating something bitter?

Tell about a bitter experience you or someone close to you had, from which you or they created good out of bitterness.

עַל אַחַת כַּמָּה וְכַמָּה טוֹבָה כְפוּלָה וּמְכֻפֶּלֶת לַמָּקוֹם עָלֵינוּ:

שֶׁהוֹצִיאָנוּ מִמִּצְרַיִם,
וְעָשָׂה בָהֶם שְׁפָטִים,
וְעָשָׂה בֵאלֹהֵיהֶם,
וְהָרַג אֶת־בְּכוֹרֵיהֶם,
וְנָתַן לָנוּ אֶת־מָמוֹנָם,
וְקָרַע לָנוּ אֶת־הַיָּם,
וְהֶעֱבִירָנוּ בְתוֹכוֹ בֶּחָרָבָה,
וְשִׁקַּע צָרֵינוּ בְּתוֹכוֹ,
וְסִפֵּק צָרְכֵּנוּ בַּמִּדְבָּר אַרְבָּעִים שָׁנָה,
וְהֶאֱכִילָנוּ אֶת־הַמָּן,
וְנָתַן לָנוּ אֶת־הַשַּׁבָּת,
וְקֵרְבָנוּ לִפְנֵי הַר סִינַי,
וְנָתַן לָנוּ אֶת־הַתּוֹרָה,
וְהִכְנִיסָנוּ לְאֶרֶץ יִשְׂרָאֵל,
וּבָנָה לָנוּ אֶת־בֵּית הַבְּחִירָה,

לְכַפֵּר עַל־כָּל־עֲוֹנוֹתֵינוּ.

רַבָּן גַּמְלִיאֵל הָיָה אוֹמֵר: כָּל שֶׁלֹּא אָמַר שְׁלֹשָׁה דְבָרִים אֵלּוּ בַּפֶּסַח, לֹא יָצָא יְדֵי חוֹבָתוֹ, וְאֵלּוּ הֵן:

פֶּסַח. מַצָּה וּמָרוֹר:

פֶּסַח שֶׁהָיוּ אֲבוֹתֵינוּ אוֹכְלִים, בִּזְמַן שֶׁבֵּית הַמִּקְדָּשׁ הָיָה קַיָּם, עַל שׁוּם מָה? עַל שׁוּם שֶׁפָּסַח הַקָּדוֹשׁ בָּרוּךְ הוּא, עַל בָּתֵּי אֲבוֹתֵינוּ בְּמִצְרַיִם, שֶׁנֶּאֱמַר:
וַאֲמַרְתֶּם זֶבַח פֶּסַח הוּא לַיְיָ, אֲשֶׁר פָּסַח עַל בָּתֵּי בְנֵי יִשְׂרָאֵל בְּמִצְרַיִם, בְּנָגְפּוֹ אֶת־מִצְרַיִם וְאֶת־בָּתֵּינוּ הִצִּיל, וַיִּקֹּד הָעָם וַיִּשְׁתַּחֲווּ.

(יגביה המצה ויאמר)

מַצָּה זוֹ שֶׁאָנוּ אוֹכְלִים, עַל שׁוּם מָה? עַל שׁוּם שֶׁלֹּא הִסְפִּיק בְּצֵקָם שֶׁל אֲבוֹתֵינוּ לְהַחֲמִיץ, עַד שֶׁנִּגְלָה עֲלֵיהֶם מֶלֶךְ מַלְכֵי הַמְּלָכִים, הַקָּדוֹשׁ בָּרוּךְ הוּא, וּגְאָלָם, שֶׁנֶּאֱמַר: וַיֹּאפוּ אֶת־הַבָּצֵק, אֲשֶׁר הוֹצִיאוּ מִמִּצְרַיִם, עֻגֹת מַצּוֹת, כִּי לֹא חָמֵץ: כִּי גֹרְשׁוּ מִמִּצְרַיִם, וְלֹא יָכְלוּ לְהִתְמַהְמֵהַּ, וְגַם צֵדָה לֹא עָשׂוּ לָהֶם.

(יגביה המרור ויאמר)

מָרוֹר זֶה שֶׁאָנוּ אוֹכְלִים, עַל שׁוּם מָה? עַל שׁוּם שֶׁמֵּרְרוּ הַמִּצְרִים אֶת־חַיֵּי אֲבוֹתֵינוּ בְּמִצְרַיִם, שֶׁנֶּאֱמַר: וַיְמָרְרוּ אֶת־חַיֵּיהֶם בַּעֲבֹדָה קָשָׁה, בְּחֹמֶר וּבִלְבֵנִים, וּבְכָל־עֲבֹדָה בַּשָּׂדֶה: אֵת כָּל־עֲבֹדָתָם, אֲשֶׁר עָבְדוּ בָהֶם בְּפָרֶךְ.

THE ROSENSTEIN HAGGADAH

In Every Generation

בְּכָל־דּוֹר וָדוֹר חַיָּב אָדָם לִרְאוֹת אֶת־עַצְמוֹ, כְּאִלּוּ הוּא יָצָא מִמִּצְרָיִם.

B'chol dor vador, chayav adam lirot et atzmo k'ilu hu yatza miMitzraim.

In every generation, each person must view himself or herself as having personally gone out of Egypt.

The phrase "in every generation" implies that we must relate the story of the Exodus to our particular circumstances. How would you say that applies today?

"…the imperative to narrate the Exodus becomes the very purpose of the historical event; it happened so that you can tell about it." [28]

The narrative reminds us of the anguish of being a stranger in the Land of Egypt, so that our mercy will be aroused for others in that situation.

שֶׁנֶּאֱמַר: וְהִגַּדְתָּ לְבִנְךָ בַּיּוֹם הַהוּא לֵאמֹר: בַּעֲבוּר זֶה עָשָׂה יְיָ לִי, בְּצֵאתִי מִמִּצְרָיִם. לֹא אֶת־אֲבוֹתֵינוּ בִּלְבָד, גָּאַל הַקָּדוֹשׁ בָּרוּךְ הוּא, אֶלָּא אַף אוֹתָנוּ גָּאַל עִמָּהֶם, שֶׁנֶּאֱמַר: וְאוֹתָנוּ הוֹצִיא מִשָּׁם, לְמַעַן הָבִיא אֹתָנוּ, לָתֶת לָנוּ אֶת־ הָאָרֶץ אֲשֶׁר נִשְׁבַּע לַאֲבֹתֵינוּ.

(יגביה הכוס, יכסה המצות ויאמר)

לְפִיכָךְ אֲנַחְנוּ חַיָּבִים לְהוֹדוֹת, לְהַלֵּל, לְשַׁבֵּחַ, לְפָאֵר, לְרוֹמֵם, לְהַדֵּר, לְבָרֵךְ, לְעַלֵּה וּלְקַלֵּס, לְמִי שֶׁעָשָׂה לַאֲבוֹתֵינוּ וְלָנוּ אֶת־כָּל־ הַנִּסִּים הָאֵלּוּ. הוֹצִיאָנוּ מֵעַבְדוּת לְחֵרוּת, מִיָּגוֹן לְשִׂמְחָה, וּמֵאֵבֶל לְיוֹם טוֹב, וּמֵאֲפֵלָה לְאוֹר גָּדוֹל, וּמִשִּׁעְבּוּד לִגְאֻלָּה.

Songs of Praise

(Lift the wine cups and recite.)

Therefore, it is our duty to thank, to praise, to laud, to glorify, to exalt, to honor, to bless, to elevate and to extol the One who performed all these miracles for our ancestors and for us.

God took us from slavery to freedom, from sadness to joy, from mourning to celebration, from darkness to light, and from subjugation to redemption.

וְנֹאמַר לְפָנָיו שִׁירָה חֲדָשָׁה. הַלְלוּיָהּ.

V'nomar l'fanav shira chadasha, Halleluyah.

Therefore let us sing a new song, Halleluyah.

הַלְלוּיָהּ. הַלְלוּ עַבְדֵי יְיָ. הַלְלוּ אֶת־שֵׁם יְיָ. יְהִי שֵׁם יְיָ מְבֹרָךְ מֵעַתָּה וְעַד עוֹלָם:

Halleluyah (2x) hallelu avdei Adonai	הַלְלוּיָהּ. הַלְלוּ עַבְדֵי יְיָ.
Halleluyah (2x) hallelu et shem Adonai	הַלְלוּיָהּ. הַלְלוּ אֶת־שֵׁם יְיָ.
Yehi shem Adonai m'vorach	יְהִי שֵׁם יְיָ מְבֹרָךְ
Me'atah v'ad olam. (Repeat last two lines.)	מֵעַתָּה וְעַד עוֹלָם:
Halleluyah	הַלְלוּיָהּ.

Give praise to Adonai.
Sing praises those who serve Adonai. Blessed is the name of Adonai now and forever.

[Traditional Text]

הַלְלוּיָהּ.הַלְלוּ עַבְדֵי יְיָ. הַלְלוּ אֶת־שֵׁם יְיָ. יְהִי שֵׁם יְיָ מְבֹרָךְ מֵעַתָּה וְעַד עוֹלָם: מִמִּזְרַח שֶׁמֶשׁ עַד מְבוֹאוֹ. מְהֻלָּל שֵׁם יְיָ. רָם עַל־כָּל־גּוֹיִם יְיָ. עַל הַשָּׁמַיִם כְּבוֹדוֹ: מִי כַּיְיָ אֱלֹהֵינוּ. הַמַּגְבִּיהִי לָשָׁבֶת: הַמַּשְׁפִּילִי לִרְאוֹת בַּשָּׁמַיִם וּבָאָרֶץ: מְקִימִי מֵעָפָר דָּל. מֵאַשְׁפֹּת יָרִים אֶבְיוֹן: לְהוֹשִׁיבִי עִם־נְדִיבִים. עִם נְדִיבֵי עַמּוֹ: מוֹשִׁיבִי עֲקֶרֶת הַבַּיִת אֵם הַבָּנִים שְׂמֵחָה. הַלְלוּיָהּ:

B'tzeit Yisrael miMitrayim	בְּצֵאת יִשְׂרָאֵל מִמִּצְרָיִם,
Bet Yaakov me'am lo'ez.	בֵּית יַעֲקֹב מֵעַם לֹעֵז:
Hay'tah Yehudah l'kadsho;	הָיְתָה יְהוּדָה לְקָדְשׁוֹ,
Yisrael mamsh'lotav.	יִשְׂרָאֵל מַמְשְׁלוֹתָיו:
Hayam ra'ah vayanos;	הַיָּם רָאָה וַיָּנֹס,
Hayarden yisov l'achor.	הַיַּרְדֵּן יִסֹּב לְאָחוֹר:
Heharim rak'du ch'eilim;	הֶהָרִים רָקְדוּ כְאֵילִים.
G'vaot kivnei tzon.	גְּבָעוֹת כִּבְנֵי־צֹאן:
Mah l'cha hayam ki tanus;	מַה־לְּךָ הַיָּם כִּי תָנוּס.
HaYarden tisov l'achor.	הַיַּרְדֵּן תִּסֹּב לְאָחוֹר:
Heharim tirk'du ch'eilim;	הֶהָרִים תִּרְקְדוּ כְאֵילִים.
G'vaot kivnei tzon.	גְּבָעוֹת כִּבְנֵי־צֹאן:
Milifnei adon chuli aretz;	מִלִּפְנֵי אָדוֹן חוּלִי אָרֶץ.
Milifnei Elohai Ya'akov.	מִלִּפְנֵי אֱלוֹהַּ יַעֲקֹב:
Hahofchi hatzur agam mayim;	הַהֹפְכִי הַצּוּר אֲגַם־מָיִם.
Chalamish l'maino mayim.	חַלָּמִישׁ לְמַעְיְנוֹ־מָיִם:

When Israel left Egypt, when the House of Jacob left these foreign people, Judah became God's holy one, Israel God's dominion. The sea fled at the sight, the Jordan River retreated. The mountains skipped like rams, the hills like lambs, before the presence of the Creator who turns rock into pools of water and flint into fountains.

(Lift the wine cups and recite.)

Blessed are You Adonai, Sovereign of the world, who has redeemed our ancestors and us from Egypt and brought us here this night to eat matzah and maror. Adonai our God, and God of our ancestors, enable us to celebrate future holidays and festivals in peace and in joy. Then we will praise You with a new song.

Baruch Atah Adonai, Ga'al Yisrael.

בָּרוּךְ אַתָּה יְיָ, אֱלֹהֵינוּ מֶלֶךְ הָעוֹלָם, אֲשֶׁר גְּאָלָנוּ וְגָאַל אֶת־אֲבוֹתֵינוּ מִמִּצְרַיִם, וְהִגִּיעָנוּ לַלַּיְלָה הַזֶּה, לֶאֱכָל־בּוֹ מַצָּה וּמָרוֹר. כֵּן, יְיָ אֱלֹהֵינוּ וֵאלֹהֵי אֲבוֹתֵינוּ, יַגִּיעֵנוּ לְמוֹעֲדִים וְלִרְגָלִים אֲחֵרִים, הַבָּאִים לִקְרָאתֵנוּ לְשָׁלוֹם. שְׂמֵחִים בְּבִנְיַן עִירֶךָ, וְשָׂשִׂים בַּעֲבוֹדָתֶךָ, וְנֹאכַל שָׁם מִן הַזְּבָחִים וּמִן הַפְּסָחִים (במוצאי שבת יש אומרים: מִן הַפְּסָחִים וּמִן הַזְּבָחִים), אֲשֶׁר יַגִּיעַ דָּמָם, עַל קִיר מִזְבַּחֲךָ לְרָצוֹן, וְנוֹדֶה לְךָ שִׁיר חָדָשׁ עַל גְּאֻלָּתֵנוּ, וְעַל פְּדוּת נַפְשֵׁנוּ: בָּרוּךְ אַתָּה יְיָ, גָּאַל יִשְׂרָאֵל:

Blessed are You, Adonai our God, Redeemer of the people Israel.

Second Cup – "I Will Rescue You."

We are now ready for the second cup of wine, which we drink while reclining.

בָּרוּךְ אַתָּה יְיָ, אֱלֹהֵינוּ מֶלֶךְ הָעוֹלָם, בּוֹרֵא פְּרִי הַגָּפֶן.

Baruch Atah Adonai, Eloheinu melech haolam, borei p'ree hagafen.

Blessed are You Adonai, Sovereign of the world, who creates the fruit of the vine.

(Drink the second cup while reclining.)

RACHTZAH

רָחְצָה

WE WASH OUR HANDS AND SAY A BLESSING

We wash our hands for the meal and recite the blessing:

בָּרוּךְ אַתָּה יְיָ אֱלֹהֵינוּ מֶלֶךְ הָעוֹלָם, אֲשֶׁר קִדְּשָׁנוּ בְּמִצְוֹתָיו, וְצִוָּנוּ עַל נְטִילַת יָדָיִם:

Baruch Atah Adonai, Eloheinu melech haolam, asher kid'shanu b'mitzvotav, v'tzivanu al n'tilat yadayim.

Blessed are You, Adonai our God, Sovereign of the world, who has made us holy through Your mitzvot, and commanded us to wash our hands.

MOTZI MATZAH

WE SAY THE BLESSING FOR "BREAD" AND MATZAH

(Distribute pieces of the upper and middle matzah.)

We recite the two blessings for "bread" and matzah:

בָּרוּךְ אַתָּה יְיָ, אֱלֹהֵינוּ מֶלֶךְ הָעוֹלָם, הַמּוֹצִיא לֶחֶם מִן הָאָרֶץ:

Baruch Atah Adonai, Eloheinu melech haolam, hamotzi lechem min ha'aretz.

Blessed are You, Adonai our God, Sovereign of the world, who brings forth bread from the earth.

בָּרוּךְ אַתָּה יְיָ, אֱלֹהֵינוּ מֶלֶךְ הָעוֹלָם, אֲשֶׁר קִדְּשָׁנוּ בְּמִצְוֹתָיו וְצִוָּנוּ עַל אֲכִילַת מַצָּה:

Baruch Atah Adonai, Eloheinu melech haolam, asher kid'shanu b'mitzvotav, v'tzivanu al achilat matzah.

Blessed are You, Adonai our God, Sovereign of the world, who made us holy by Your mitzvot and commanded us to eat matzah.

(Eat the matzah.)

In Exodus we are told, "You shall guard the matzah." This means that when we prepare matzah, we watch that it not become sour, hence rising through the souring process.²⁹

Another interpretation is that "guarding the matzah" refers to the person who performs the mitzvah of eating matzah, which should be done with joy and celebration and not with a "sour face."³⁰

MAROR

DIP THE BITTER HERB

(Give everyone a piece of maror and some charoset.)

Ashkenazim usually eat horseradish for maror. Sephardim and Mizrachim (Eastern) Jews usually eat romaine, endive lettuce, or escarole. We dip the maror into the charoset to acknowledge that our bitterness was sweetened by our redemption.

בָּרוּךְ אַתָּה יְיָ אֱלֹהֵינוּ מֶלֶךְ הָעוֹלָם, אֲשֶׁר קִדְּשָׁנוּ בְּמִצְוֹתָיו וְצִוָּנוּ עַל אֲכִילַת מָרוֹר:

Baruch Atah Adonai, Eloheinu melech haolam, asher kid'shanu b'mitzvotav, v'tzivanu al achilat maror.

Blessed are You, Adonai our God, Sovereign of the world, who made us holy by Your mitzvot, and commanded us to eat maror.

About Charoset

In Gibraltar, Jews put the dust of bricks into their charoset dish, to symbolize the bricks the Israelites used for the buildings they were forced to make.[31]

During the American Civil War, a group of Jewish Union Soldiers, not having ingredients for charoset, put a real brick in its place on the Seder Plate.[32]

Despite being a part of our Seder because of its sweetness, charoset also reminds us of the mixture the Israelites made for bricks to build cities for the Pharaoh. Do you think charoset can stand for two incongruous things?

Eating charoset was ruled not to be a part of the religious ceremony, but Rabbi Levi argued that it should be, in memory of the apple trees under which the Israelite women gave birth during the period of slavery. Can you think of other examples in our history when Jews did life - affirming actions despite horrific circumstances?

THE ROSENSTEIN HAGGADAH

KORECH

EAT A SANDWICH WITH MATZAH AND MAROR

(Distribute pieces of maror and pieces of the bottom matzah.)

We do as the sage Hillel did in Temple times. He would make a sandwich of the Pesach (lamb offering) with the matzah and maror. Since we no longer bring sacrifices, our sandwich only has matzah and maror.

(Eat the Hillel sandwich.)

זֵכֶר לְמִקְדָּשׁ כְּהִלֵּל: כֵּן עָשָׂה הִלֵּל בִּזְמַן שֶׁבֵּית הַמִּקְדָּשׁ הָיָה קַיָּם. הָיָה כּוֹרֵךְ פֶּסַח מַצָּה וּמָרוֹר וְאוֹכֵל בְּיַחַד. לְקַיֵּם מַה שֶׁנֶּאֱמַר: עַל־מַצּוֹת וּמְרוֹרִים יֹאכְלֻהוּ:

Once a pagan asked Hillel to teach him the Torah while he stood on one foot. Hillel answered kindly, "That which is hateful to you, do not do to your neighbor. That is the whole Torah. All the rest is commentary; now go and learn."

EGGS

You may have heard any of the following explanations for why we eat eggs at the beginning of the Seder meal: They are a symbol of life. They are a symbol of the Temple sacrifice. They remind us that God has no beginning or end. They are a symbol of springtime and rebirth. They remind us of the midwives, Shifrah and Puah, who with courage and creativity saved Hebrew baby boys from death. You may be surprised that none of these explanations appear in the Torah or Babylonian Talmud. They are relatively new.[42] Can you think of another interpretation of why we eat eggs?

SHULCHAN ORECH

שֻׁלְחָן עוֹרֵךְ

WE EAT THE MEAL

TZAFUN

WE EAT THE AFIKOMEN

After the Afikomen is found or ransomed, it is shared with all participants, as the Pesach offering was shared in the time of the Temple. No special blessing is said because the Afikomen, the dessert matzah, is part of the meal. We eat it reclining and without delay. We are not allowed to eat anything after the Afikomen, since its taste must linger in our mouths.

The word *afikomen* is derived from the Greek word *epicumen*, which means a food eaten for pleasure or a dessert. The afikomen should leave us with a lingering taste that captures all that we have derived from the meal. Do you think matzah was a good choice for the afikomen?

After the meal, we taste a piece of the afikomen, the larger piece of the middle matzah, to confirm our belief that completeness will come in the future, according to God's promise.

Why do we hide the Afikomen?

- So no one will eat it before it is time to be used as the dessert of the Seder meal
- To symbolically destroy the evil hidden inside our hearts
- To keep the children awake as long as possible

BARECH

Just as we begin eating with a blessing, so we end the meal with gratitude. As it is written, "You ate, you were satisfied, and you blessed." Deuteronomy 8:10

WE SAY THE BLESSING AFTER THE MEAL

(Pour the third cup of wine.)

(This is an abbreviated version of the Blessing After Meals.)

בָּרוּךְ אַתָּה יְיָ, אֱלֹהֵינוּ מֶלֶךְ הָעוֹלָם, הַזָּן אֶת הָעוֹלָם כֻּלּוֹ בְּטוּבוֹ בְּחֵן בְּחֶסֶד וּבְרַחֲמִים הוּא נוֹתֵן לֶחֶם לְכָל בָּשָׂר כִּי לְעוֹלָם חַסְדּוֹ. וּבְטוּבוֹ הַגָּדוֹל תָּמִיד לֹא חָסַר לָנוּ, וְאַל יֶחְסַר לָנוּ מָזוֹן לְעוֹלָם וָעֶד. בַּעֲבוּר שְׁמוֹ הַגָּדוֹל, כִּי הוּא אֵל זָן וּמְפַרְנֵס לַכֹּל וּמֵטִיב לַכֹּל, וּמֵכִין מָזוֹן לְכֹל בְּרִיּוֹתָיו אֲשֶׁר בָּרָא. בָּרוּךְ אַתָּה יְיָ, הַזָּן אֶת הַכֹּל.

עֹשֶׂה שָׁלוֹם בִּמְרוֹמָיו, הוּא יַעֲשֶׂה שָׁלוֹם, עָלֵינוּ וְעַל כָּל יִשְׂרָאֵל, וְאִמְרוּ אָמֵן.

Baruch Atah Adonai Eloheinu melech ha'olam, hazan et ha'olam kulo b'tuvo b'chen b'chesed uv'rachamin. Hu noten lechem l'chol basar ki l'olam chasdo. Uv'tuvo hagadol tamid lo chasar lanu v'al yech'sar lanu mazon l'olam va'ed. Ba'avur sh'mo hagadol ki hu zan um'farnes lakol umetiv lakol umechin mazon l'chol b'riyotav asher bara. Baruch Atah Adonai hazan et hakol.

Blessed are You, Adonai our God, Sovereign of the world, who in goodness, mercy and kindness gives food to the world. Your love for us endures forever. We praise You Adonai, who provides sustenance for all life.

May the One who makes peace in the heavens, make peace for us, for Israel, and for all humanity.

(On the next two pages is a complete Birkat HaMazon.)

שִׁיר הַמַּעֲלוֹת בְּשׁוּב יְיָ אֶת שִׁיבַת צִיּוֹן הָיִינוּ כְּחֹלְמִים: אָז יִמָּלֵא שְׂחוֹק פִּינוּ וּלְשׁוֹנֵנוּ רִנָּה אָז יֹאמְרוּ בַגּוֹיִם הִגְדִּיל יְיָ לַעֲשׂוֹת עִם אֵלֶּה: הִגְדִּיל יְיָ לַעֲשׂוֹת עִמָּנוּ הָיִינוּ שְׂמֵחִים: שׁוּבָה יְיָ אֶת שְׁבִיתֵנוּ כַּאֲפִיקִים בַּנֶּגֶב: הַזּוֹרְעִים בְּדִמְעָה בְּרִנָּה יִקְצֹרוּ: הָלוֹךְ יֵלֵךְ וּבָכֹה נֹשֵׂא מֶשֶׁךְ הַזָּרַע בֹּא יָבֹא בְרִנָּה נֹשֵׂא אֲלֻמֹּתָיו:

רַבּוֹתַי נְבָרֵךְ!
יְהִי שֵׁם יְיָ מְבֹרָךְ מֵעַתָּה וְעַד עוֹלָם.
יְהִי שֵׁם יְיָ מְבֹרָךְ מֵעַתָּה וְעַד עוֹלָם. בִּרְשׁוּת מָרָנָן וְרַבָּנָן וְרַבּוֹתַי, נְבָרֵךְ (אֱלֹהֵינוּ) שֶׁאָכַלְנוּ מִשֶּׁלּוֹ.
בָּרוּךְ (אֱלֹהֵינוּ) שֶׁאָכַלְנוּ מִשֶּׁלּוֹ וּבְטוּבוֹ חָיִינוּ.
בָּרוּךְ (אֱלֹהֵינוּ) שֶׁאָכַלְנוּ מִשֶּׁלּוֹ וּבְטוּבוֹ חָיִינוּ.

בָּרוּךְ הוּא וּבָרוּךְ שְׁמוֹ:
בָּרוּךְ אַתָּה יְיָ, אֱלֹהֵינוּ מֶלֶךְ הָעוֹלָם, הַזָּן אֶת הָעוֹלָם כֻּלּוֹ בְּטוּבוֹ בְּחֵן בְּחֶסֶד וּבְרַחֲמִים הוּא נוֹתֵן לֶחֶם לְכָל בָּשָׂר כִּי לְעוֹלָם חַסְדּוֹ. וּבְטוּבוֹ הַגָּדוֹל תָּמִיד לֹא חָסַר לָנוּ, וְאַל יֶחְסַר לָנוּ מָזוֹן לְעוֹלָם וָעֶד. בַּעֲבוּר שְׁמוֹ הַגָּדוֹל, כִּי הוּא אֵל זָן וּמְפַרְנֵס לַכֹּל וּמֵטִיב לַכֹּל, וּמֵכִין מָזוֹן לְכָל בְּרִיּוֹתָיו אֲשֶׁר בָּרָא. בָּרוּךְ אַתָּה יְיָ, הַזָּן אֶת הַכֹּל:

נוֹדֶה לְךָ יְיָ אֱלֹהֵינוּ עַל שֶׁהִנְחַלְתָּ לַאֲבוֹתֵינוּ, אֶרֶץ חֶמְדָּה טוֹבָה וּרְחָבָה, וְעַל שֶׁהוֹצֵאתָנוּ יְיָ אֱלֹהֵינוּ מֵאֶרֶץ מִצְרַיִם, וּפְדִיתָנוּ, מִבֵּית עֲבָדִים, וְעַל בְּרִיתְךָ שֶׁחָתַמְתָּ בִּבְשָׂרֵנוּ, וְעַל תּוֹרָתְךָ שֶׁלִּמַּדְתָּנוּ, וְעַל חֻקֶּיךָ שֶׁהוֹדַעְתָּנוּ, וְעַל חַיִּים חֵן וָחֶסֶד שֶׁחוֹנַנְתָּנוּ, וְעַל אֲכִילַת מָזוֹן שָׁאַתָּה זָן וּמְפַרְנֵס אוֹתָנוּ תָּמִיד, בְּכָל יוֹם וּבְכָל עֵת וּבְכָל שָׁעָה:

וְעַל הַכֹּל יְיָ אֱלֹהֵינוּ אֲנַחְנוּ מוֹדִים לָךְ, וּמְבָרְכִים אוֹתָךְ, יִתְבָּרַךְ שִׁמְךָ בְּפִי כָּל חַי תָּמִיד לְעוֹלָם וָעֶד. כַּכָּתוּב, וְאָכַלְתָּ וְשָׂבָעְתָּ, וּבֵרַכְתָּ אֶת יְיָ אֱלֹהֶיךָ עַל הָאָרֶץ הַטֹּבָה אֲשֶׁר נָתַן לָךְ. בָּרוּךְ אַתָּה יְיָ, עַל הָאָרֶץ וְעַל הַמָּזוֹן:

רַחֵם נָא יְיָ אֱלֹהֵינוּ, עַל יִשְׂרָאֵל עַמֶּךָ, וְעַל יְרוּשָׁלַיִם עִירֶךָ, וְעַל צִיּוֹן מִשְׁכַּן כְּבוֹדֶךָ, וְעַל מַלְכוּת בֵּית דָּוִד מְשִׁיחֶךָ, וְעַל הַבַּיִת הַגָּדוֹל וְהַקָּדוֹשׁ שֶׁנִּקְרָא שִׁמְךָ עָלָיו. אֱלֹהֵינוּ, אָבִינוּ, רְעֵנוּ, זוּנֵנוּ, פַּרְנְסֵנוּ, וְכַלְכְּלֵנוּ, וְהַרְוִיחֵנוּ, וְהַרְוַח לָנוּ יְיָ אֱלֹהֵינוּ מְהֵרָה מִכָּל צָרוֹתֵינוּ, וְנָא, אַל תַּצְרִיכֵנוּ יְיָ אֱלֹהֵינוּ, לֹא לִידֵי מַתְּנַת בָּשָׂר וָדָם, וְלֹא לִידֵי הַלְוָאָתָם. כִּי אִם לְיָדְךָ הַמְּלֵאָה, הַפְּתוּחָה, הַקְּדוֹשָׁה וְהָרְחָבָה, שֶׁלֹּא נֵבוֹשׁ וְלֹא נִכָּלֵם לְעוֹלָם וָעֶד:

לשבת רְצֵה וְהַחֲלִיצֵנוּ יְיָ אֱלֹהֵינוּ בְּמִצְוֹתֶיךָ וּבְמִצְוַת יוֹם הַשְּׁבִיעִי הַשַּׁבָּת הַגָּדוֹל וְהַקָּדוֹשׁ הַזֶּה. כִּי יוֹם זֶה גָּדוֹל וְקָדוֹשׁ הוּא לְפָנֶיךָ, לִשְׁבָּת בּוֹ וְלָנוּחַ בּוֹ בְּאַהֲבָה כְּמִצְוַת רְצוֹנֶךָ וּבִרְצוֹנְךָ הָנִיחַ לָנוּ יְיָ אֱלֹהֵינוּ, שֶׁלֹּא תְהֵא צָרָה וְיָגוֹן וַאֲנָחָה בְּיוֹם מְנוּחָתֵנוּ. וְהַרְאֵנוּ יְיָ אֱלֹהֵינוּ בְּנֶחָמַת צִיּוֹן עִירֶךָ, וּבְבִנְיַן יְרוּשָׁלַיִם עִיר קָדְשֶׁךָ, כִּי אַתָּה הוּא בַּעַל הַיְשׁוּעוֹת וּבַעַל הַנֶּחָמוֹת:

אֱלֹהֵינוּ וֵאלֹהֵי אֲבוֹתֵינוּ, יַעֲלֶה וְיָבֹא וְיַגִּיעַ, וְיֵרָאֶה, וְיֵרָצֶה, וְיִשָּׁמַע, וְיִפָּקֵד, וְיִזָּכֵר זִכְרוֹנֵנוּ וּפִקְדוֹנֵנוּ, וְזִכְרוֹן אֲבוֹתֵינוּ, וְזִכְרוֹן מָשִׁיחַ בֶּן דָּוִד עַבְדֶּךָ, וְזִכְרוֹן יְרוּשָׁלַיִם עִיר קָדְשֶׁךָ, וְזִכְרוֹן כָּל עַמְּךָ בֵּית יִשְׂרָאֵל לְפָנֶיךָ, לִפְלֵיטָה לְטוֹבָה לְחֵן וּלְחֶסֶד וּלְרַחֲמִים, לְחַיִּים וּלְשָׁלוֹם בְּיוֹם חַג הַמַּצּוֹת הַזֶּה. זָכְרֵנוּ יְיָ אֱלֹהֵינוּ בּוֹ לְטוֹבָה. וּפָקְדֵנוּ בוֹ לִבְרָכָה. וְהוֹשִׁיעֵנוּ בוֹ לְחַיִּים, וּבִדְבַר יְשׁוּעָה וְרַחֲמִים, חוּס וְחָנֵּנוּ, וְרַחֵם עָלֵינוּ וְהוֹשִׁיעֵנוּ, כִּי אֵלֶיךָ עֵינֵינוּ, כִּי אֵל מֶלֶךְ חַנּוּן וְרַחוּם אָתָּה:

וּבְנֵה יְרוּשָׁלַיִם עִיר הַקֹּדֶשׁ בִּמְהֵרָה בְיָמֵינוּ. בָּרוּךְ אַתָּה יְיָ, בּוֹנֶה בְרַחֲמָיו יְרוּשָׁלָיִם. אָמֵן

בָּרוּךְ אַתָּה יְיָ אֱלֹהֵינוּ מֶלֶךְ הָעוֹלָם, הָאֵל אָבִינוּ, מַלְכֵּנוּ, אַדִירֵנוּ בּוֹרְאֵנוּ, גּוֹאֲלֵנוּ, יוֹצְרֵנוּ, קְדוֹשֵׁנוּ קְדוֹשׁ יַעֲקֹב, רוֹעֵנוּ רוֹעֵה יִשְׂרָאֵל. הַמֶּלֶךְ הַטּוֹב, וְהַמֵּטִיב לַכֹּל, שֶׁבְּכָל יוֹם וָיוֹם הוּא הֵטִיב, הוּא מֵטִיב, הוּא יֵיטִיב לָנוּ. הוּא גְמָלָנוּ, הוּא גוֹמְלֵנוּ, הוּא יִגְמְלֵנוּ לָעַד לְחֵן וּלְחֶסֶד וּלְרַחֲמִים וּלְרֶוַח הַצָּלָה וְהַצְלָחָה בְּרָכָה וִישׁוּעָה, נֶחָמָה, פַּרְנָסָה וְכַלְכָּלָה, וְרַחֲמִים, וְחַיִּים וְשָׁלוֹם, וְכָל טוֹב, וּמִכָּל טוּב לְעוֹלָם אַל יְחַסְּרֵנוּ:

הָרַחֲמָן, הוּא יִמְלוֹךְ עָלֵינוּ לְעוֹלָם וָעֶד.

הָרַחֲמָן, הוּא יִתְבָּרַךְ בַּשָּׁמַיִם וּבָאָרֶץ.

הָרַחֲמָן, הוּא יִשְׁתַּבַּח לְדוֹר דּוֹרִים, וְיִתְפָּאַר בָּנוּ לָעַד וּלְנֵצַח נְצָחִים, וְיִתְהַדַּר בָּנוּ לָעַד וּלְעוֹלְמֵי עוֹלָמִים.

הָרַחֲמָן, הוּא יְפַרְנְסֵנוּ בְּכָבוֹד.

הָרַחֲמָן, הוּא יִשְׁבּוֹר עֻלֵּנוּ מֵעַל צַוָּארֵנוּ וְהוּא יוֹלִיכֵנוּ קוֹמְמִיּוּת לְאַרְצֵנוּ.

הָרַחֲמָן, הוּא יִשְׁלַח לָנוּ בְּרָכָה מְרֻבָּה בַּבַּיִת הַזֶּה, וְעַל שֻׁלְחָן זֶה שֶׁאָכַלְנוּ עָלָיו.

הָרַחֲמָן, הוּא יִשְׁלַח לָנוּ אֶת אֵלִיָּהוּ הַנָּבִיא זָכוּר לַטּוֹב, וִיבַשֶּׂר לָנוּ בְּשׂוֹרוֹת טוֹבוֹת יְשׁוּעוֹת וְנֶחָמוֹת.

הָרַחֲמָן, הוּא יְבָרֵךְ אֶת (אָבִי מוֹרִי) בַּעַל הַבַּיִת הַזֶּה, וְאֶת (אִמִּי מוֹרָתִי) בַּעֲלַת הַבַּיִת הַזֶּה,

הָרַחֲמָן, הוּא יְבָרֵךְ אוֹתִי (וְאָבִי וְאִמִּי וְאִשְׁתִּי וְזַרְעִי וְאֶת כָּל אֲשֶׁר לִי)

הָרַחֲמָן, הוּא יְבָרֵךְ אֶת בַּעַל הַבַּיִת הַזֶּה, וְאֶת אִשְׁתּוֹ בַּעֲלַת הַבַּיִת הַזֶּה.

אוֹתָם וְאֶת בֵּיתָם וְאֶת זַרְעָם וְאֶת כָּל אֲשֶׁר לָהֶם אוֹתָנוּ וְאֶת כָּל אֲשֶׁר לָנוּ, כְּמוֹ שֶׁנִּתְבָּרְכוּ אֲבוֹתֵינוּ, אַבְרָהָם יִצְחָק וְיַעֲקֹב: בַּכֹּל, מִכֹּל, כֹּל. כֵּן יְבָרֵךְ אוֹתָנוּ כֻּלָּנוּ יַחַד. בִּבְרָכָה שְׁלֵמָה, וְנֹאמַר אָמֵן:

בַּמָּרוֹם יְלַמְּדוּ עֲלֵיהֶם וְעָלֵינוּ זְכוּת, שֶׁתְּהֵא לְמִשְׁמֶרֶת שָׁלוֹם, וְנִשָּׂא בְרָכָה מֵאֵת יְיָ וּצְדָקָה מֵאֱלֹהֵי יִשְׁעֵנוּ, וְנִמְצָא חֵן וְשֵׂכֶל טוֹב בְּעֵינֵי אֱלֹהִים וְאָדָם:

לשבת הָרַחֲמָן, הוּא יַנְחִילֵנוּ יוֹם שֶׁכֻּלּוֹ שַׁבָּת וּמְנוּחָה לְחַיֵּי הָעוֹלָמִים.

הָרַחֲמָן, הוּא יַנְחִילֵנוּ יוֹם שֶׁכֻּלּוֹ טוֹב.

הָרַחֲמָן, הוּא יְזַכֵּנוּ לִימוֹת הַמָּשִׁיחַ וּלְחַיֵּי הָעוֹלָם הַבָּא. מִגְדּוֹל יְשׁוּעוֹת מַלְכּוֹ, וְעֹשֶׂה חֶסֶד לִמְשִׁיחוֹ לְדָוִד וּלְזַרְעוֹ עַד עוֹלָם: עֹשֶׂה שָׁלוֹם בִּמְרוֹמָיו, הוּא יַעֲשֶׂה שָׁלוֹם, עָלֵינוּ וְעַל כָּל יִשְׂרָאֵל, וְאִמְרוּ אָמֵן:

יְראוּ אֶת יְיָ קְדוֹשָׁיו, כִּי אֵין מַחְסוֹר לִירֵאָיו: כְּפִירִים רָשׁוּ וְרָעֵבוּ, וְדוֹרְשֵׁי יְיָ לֹא יַחְסְרוּ כָל טוֹב: הוֹדוּ לַייָ כִּי טוֹב, כִּי לְעוֹלָם חַסְדּוֹ: פּוֹתֵחַ אֶת יָדֶךָ, וּמַשְׂבִּיעַ לְכָל חַי רָצוֹן: בָּרוּךְ הַגֶּבֶר אֲשֶׁר יִבְטַח בַּייָ, וְהָיָה יְיָ מִבְטַחוֹ: נַעַר הָיִיתִי גַם זָקַנְתִּי וְלֹא רָאִיתִי צַדִּיק נֶעֱזָב, וְזַרְעוֹ מְבַקֶּשׁ לָחֶם: יְיָ עֹז לְעַמּוֹ יִתֵּן, יְיָ יְבָרֵךְ אֶת עַמּוֹ בַשָּׁלוֹם:

The Third Cup – " I Will Redeem You."

(Lift the wine cups.)

We are now ready for the third cup of wine, which we drink while reclining.

בָּרוּךְ אַתָּה יְיָ, אֱלֹהֵינוּ מֶלֶךְ הָעוֹלָם, בּוֹרֵא פְּרִי הַגָּפֶן:

Baruch Atah Adonai, Eloheinu melech haolam, borai p'ree hagafen.

Blessed are You, Adonai our God, Sovereign of the world, who creates the fruit of the vine.

(Drink the third cup while reclining.)

Pour Out Your Wrath

(Some open the door at this point and close it after the recitation.)

We express our anxieties and trepidation about those now involved in evil. We ask God to deal with them accordingly and hope we ourselves will be spared confrontation.

שְׁפֹךְ חֲמָתְךָ אֶל־הַגּוֹיִם, אֲשֶׁר לֹא יְדָעוּךָ וְעַל־מַמְלָכוֹת אֲשֶׁר בְּשִׁמְךָ לֹא קָרָאוּ: כִּי אָכַל אֶת־יַעֲקֹב. וְאֶת־נָוֵהוּ הֵשַׁמּוּ: שְׁפָךְ־עֲלֵיהֶם זַעְמֶךָ, וַחֲרוֹן אַפְּךָ יַשִּׂיגֵם: תִּרְדֹּף בְּאַף וְתַשְׁמִידֵם, מִתַּחַת שְׁמֵי יְיָ:

Pour out Your wrath on the nations that do not recognize You or do not invoke Your name. For they have destroyed Jacob and his habitation. (Some Sephardic texts stop here.) Pour forth Your indignation and let Your burning anger overtake the wicked. Pursue them and obliterate them.

In a medieval Haggadah from Worms, next to *Pour Out Your Wrath*, *A Pour Out Your Love* prayer was found. We too can pray for love to be bestowed to all who have extended love to the Jewish people. To whom would you want to express great love?

When should we give up our anger and when should we not?

Welcoming Miriam

(Pour a cup of water and put it in the center of the table.)

We drink from the prophet Miriam's cup to symbolize the sustaining waters of her wisdom and healing. We look to her for spiritual guidance to inspire us to celebrate our blessings and work for tikun olam, the repair of the world.

Miriam ha nevi'ah oz v'zimrah beyadah,
Miriam tirkod itanu l'takein et haolam. (2x)
Bimherah v'yameinu hi tevi'enu
El mei hayeshuah. (2x).[48]

מִרְיָם הַנְּבִיאָה עֹז וְזִמְרָה בְּיָדָהּ.
מִרְיָם תִּרְקוֹד אִתָּנוּ
לְהַגְדִּיל זִמְרַת עוֹלָם
מִרְיָם תִּרְקוֹד אִתָּנוּ
לְתַקֵּן אֶת־הָעוֹלָם.
בִּמְהֵרָה בְיָמֵינוּ הִיא תְּבִיאֵנוּ
אֶל מֵי הַיְשׁוּעָה.

Miriam, the prophet,
Dance with us to repair the world.
Bring us soon, your healing waters.

Miriam's Cup represents the living waters that sustained the Hebrews through the wilderness. These were given to the people due to Miriam's merit. Miriam's Well was said to have had healing powers that not only refreshed their bodies, but also renewed their souls. We look to Miriam—prophet, poet, leader, and healer—as a role model, a guide on our spiritual journeys.

Share what nourishes you spiritually.

THE ROSENSTEIN HAGGADAH

Welcoming Elijah

(Pour a cup of wine for Elijah and place it next to Miriam's Cup at the center of the table.)

(Some follow the custom of having all Seder participants pour a little wine from their cups into Elijah's cup, to indicate that each of us must contribute to the effort to redeem the world. Most Sephardim do not have a custom of opening the door for Elijah.)

This cup is for Elijah the prophet. We open the door to greet him and invite him to join us. We pray that he will return to us soon, bringing a time of freedom, justice and peace for the entire world.

אֵלִיָּהוּ הַנָּבִיא, אֵלִיָּהוּ הַתִּשְׁבִּי,
אֵלִיָּהוּ, אֵלִיָּהוּ, אֵלִיָּהוּ הַגִּלְעָדִי,
בִּמְהֵרָה בְיָמֵינוּ יָבֹא אֵלֵינוּ עִם מָשִׁיחַ בֶּן דָּוִד.

Eliyahu hanavi, Eliyahu haTishbi,
Eliyahu, Eliyahu, Eliyahu, haGiladi.
Bimheira v'yameinu, yavo eleinu
im Mashiach ben David. (2x)

May the prophet Elijah, come to us quickly and in our day, bringing the time of Messiah.

Sephardic Jews do not usually have a cup for Elijah. It is mostly an Ashkenazic custom. In Casablanca, Moroccan Jews would have an elaborately decorated chair to welcome the prophet.[33]

The prophet Elijah was a serious advocate for living a moral life. It is said that he sometimes returns disguised as a beggar, to see how we would treat him. Thus he judges whether we are ready for the Messianic age.

According to the prophet Malachi, Elijah will, "reconcile the hearts of the children with the hearts of their parents." What issues in our time do you think need reconciliation?

HALLEL

HALLEL

WE SING SONGS OF PRAISE

Selected verses from Hallel

God will bless the House of Israel.
God will bless the House of Aaron.
God will bless those who are reverent, young and old alike.

The dead cannot praise God,
nor can those who go down into silence.
But, we shall praise God, now and always.
Halleluyah!

I love to know that God hears my cries.
Because God listens, I will cry out, all the days of my life.

How can I repay God for all the gifts to me?
I will raise the cup of deliverance, and call God by name.
My vows to God will I repay in the presence of all the people.

Thank God for great kindness; God's love endures forever.

Open the gates of righteousness for me,
that I may enter and thank God.
This is the gate of God, the righteous shall
enter here.

This is the day God made;
Let us all rejoice!

HALLEL

לֹא לָנוּ יְיָ לֹא לָנוּ   כִּי לְשִׁמְךָ תֵּן כָּבוֹד,
עַל חַסְדְּךָ עַל אֲמִתֶּךָ.

לָמָּה יֹאמְרוּ הַגּוֹיִם,   אַיֵּה נָא אֱלֹהֵיהֶם.
וֵאלֹהֵינוּ בַשָּׁמַיִם   כֹּל אֲשֶׁר חָפֵץ עָשָׂה.
עֲצַבֵּיהֶם כֶּסֶף וְזָהָב,   מַעֲשֵׂה יְדֵי אָדָם.
פֶּה לָהֶם וְלֹא יְדַבֵּרוּ,   עֵינַיִם לָהֶם וְלֹא יִרְאוּ.
אָזְנַיִם לָהֶם וְלֹא יִשְׁמָעוּ,   אַף לָהֶם וְלֹא יְרִיחוּן.
יְדֵיהֶם וְלֹא יְמִישׁוּן,   רַגְלֵיהֶם וְלֹא יְהַלֵּכוּ,
לֹא יֶהְגּוּ בִּגְרוֹנָם.

כְּמוֹהֶם יִהְיוּ עֹשֵׂיהֶם,   כֹּל אֲשֶׁר בֹּטֵחַ בָּהֶם:
יִשְׂרָאֵל בְּטַח בַּיְיָ,   עֶזְרָם וּמָגִנָּם הוּא.
בֵּית אַהֲרֹן בִּטְחוּ בַיְיָ,   עֶזְרָם וּמָגִנָּם הוּא.
יִרְאֵי יְיָ בִּטְחוּ בַיְיָ,   עֶזְרָם וּמָגִנָּם הוּא.

יְיָ זְכָרָנוּ יְבָרֵךְ,   יְבָרֵךְ אֶת בֵּית יִשְׂרָאֵל,
יְבָרֵךְ אֶת בֵּית אַהֲרֹן.
יְבָרֵךְ יִרְאֵי יְיָ,   הַקְּטַנִּים עִם הַגְּדֹלִים.
יֹסֵף יְיָ עֲלֵיכֶם,   עֲלֵיכֶם וְעַל בְּנֵיכֶם.
בְּרוּכִים אַתֶּם לַיְיָ,   עֹשֵׂה שָׁמַיִם וָאָרֶץ.
הַשָּׁמַיִם שָׁמַיִם לַיְיָ,   וְהָאָרֶץ נָתַן לִבְנֵי אָדָם.
לֹא הַמֵּתִים יְהַלְלוּ יָהּ,   וְלֹא כָּל יֹרְדֵי דוּמָה.
וַאֲנַחְנוּ נְבָרֵךְ יָהּ,   מֵעַתָּה וְעַד עוֹלָם, הַלְלוּיָהּ:

אָהַבְתִּי כִּי יִשְׁמַע יְיָ,   אֶת קוֹלִי תַּחֲנוּנָי.
כִּי הִטָּה אָזְנוֹ לִי   וּבְיָמַי אֶקְרָא:
אֲפָפוּנִי חֶבְלֵי מָוֶת,   וּמְצָרֵי שְׁאוֹל מְצָאוּנִי
צָרָה וְיָגוֹן אֶמְצָא.

וּבְשֵׁם יְיָ אֶקְרָא,   אָנָּה יְיָ מַלְּטָה נַפְשִׁי.
חַנּוּן יְיָ וְצַדִּיק,   וֵאלֹהֵינוּ מְרַחֵם.
שֹׁמֵר פְּתָאיִם יְיָ   דַּלּוֹתִי וְלִי יְהוֹשִׁיעַ.

HALLEL

שׁוּבִי נַפְשִׁי לִמְנוּחָיְכִי,	כִּי יְיָ גָּמַל עָלָיְכִי.
כִּי חִלַּצְתָּ נַפְשִׁי מִמָּוֶת	אֶת עֵינִי מִן דִּמְעָה,
אֶת רַגְלִי מִדֶּחִי.	
אֶתְהַלֵּךְ לִפְנֵי יְיָ,	בְּאַרְצוֹת הַחַיִּים.
הֶאֱמַנְתִּי כִּי אֲדַבֵּר,	אֲנִי עָנִיתִי מְאֹד.
אֲנִי אָמַרְתִּי בְחָפְזִי	כָּל הָאָדָם כֹּזֵב.
מָה אָשִׁיב לַייָ,	כָּל תַּגְמוּלוֹהִי עָלָי.
כּוֹס יְשׁוּעוֹת אֶשָּׂא,	וּבְשֵׁם יְיָ אֶקְרָא.
נְדָרַי לַייָ אֲשַׁלֵּם,	נֶגְדָה נָּא לְכָל עַמּוֹ.
יָקָר בְּעֵינֵי יְיָ	הַמָּוְתָה לַחֲסִידָיו.
אָנָּה יְיָ כִּי אֲנִי עַבְדֶּךָ	אֲנִי עַבְדְּךָ, בֶּן אֲמָתֶךָ
פִּתַּחְתָּ לְמוֹסֵרָי.	
לְךָ אֶזְבַּח זֶבַח תּוֹדָה	וּבְשֵׁם יְיָ אֶקְרָא.
נְדָרַי לַייָ אֲשַׁלֵּם	נֶגְדָה נָּא לְכָל עַמּוֹ.
בְּחַצְרוֹת בֵּית יְיָ	בְּתוֹכֵכִי יְרוּשָׁלָיִם הַלְלוּיָהּ.
הַלְלוּ אֶת יְיָ, כָּל גּוֹיִם,	שַׁבְּחוּהוּ כָּל הָאֻמִּים.
כִּי גָבַר עָלֵינוּ חַסְדּוֹ,	וֶאֱמֶת יְיָ לְעוֹלָם הַלְלוּיָהּ:
הוֹדוּ לַייָ כִּי טוֹב,	כִּי לְעוֹלָם חַסְדּוֹ:
יֹאמַר נָא יִשְׂרָאֵל,	כִּי לְעוֹלָם חַסְדּוֹ:
יֹאמְרוּ נָא בֵית אַהֲרֹן,	כִּי לְעוֹלָם חַסְדּוֹ:
יֹאמְרוּ נָא יִרְאֵי יְיָ,	כִּי לְעוֹלָם חַסְדּוֹ:
מִן הַמֵּצַר קָרָאתִי יָּהּ,	עָנָנִי בַמֶּרְחָב יָהּ.
יְיָ לִי לֹא אִירָא,	מַה יַּעֲשֶׂה לִי אָדָם.
יְיָ לִי בְּעֹזְרָי,	וַאֲנִי אֶרְאֶה בְשֹׂנְאָי.
טוֹב לַחֲסוֹת בַּייָ,	מִבְּטֹחַ בָּאָדָם.
טוֹב לַחֲסוֹת בַּייָ	מִבְּטֹחַ בִּנְדִיבִים.
כָּל גּוֹיִם סְבָבוּנִי	בְּשֵׁם יְיָ כִּי אֲמִילַם.
סַבּוּנִי גַם סְבָבוּנִי	בְּשֵׁם יְיָ כִּי אֲמִילַם.
סַבּוּנִי כִדְבֹרִים	דֹּעֲכוּ כְּאֵשׁ קוֹצִים,

HALLEL

בְּשֵׁם יְיָ כִּי אֲמִילָם.

דָּחֹה דְחִיתַנִי לִנְפֹּל,   וַיְיָ עֲזָרָנִי.
עָזִּי וְזִמְרָת יָהּ,   וַיְהִי לִי לִישׁוּעָה.
קוֹל רִנָּה וִישׁוּעָה   בְּאָהֳלֵי צַדִּיקִים,

יְמִין יְיָ עֹשָׂה חָיִל.

יְמִין יְיָ רוֹמֵמָה,   יְמִין יְיָ עֹשָׂה חָיִל.
לֹא אָמוּת כִּי אֶחְיֶה,   וַאֲסַפֵּר מַעֲשֵׂי יָהּ.
יַסֹּר יִסְּרַנִּי יָּהּ,   וְלַמָּוֶת לֹא נְתָנָנִי.
פִּתְחוּ לִי שַׁעֲרֵי צֶדֶק,   אָבֹא בָם אוֹדֶה יָהּ.
זֶה הַשַּׁעַר לַיְיָ,   צַדִּיקִים יָבֹאוּ בוֹ.
אוֹדְךָ כִּי עֲנִיתָנִי,   וַתְּהִי לִי לִישׁוּעָה.
אוֹדְךָ כִּי עֲנִיתָנִי,   וַתְּהִי לִי לִישׁוּעָה.
אֶבֶן מָאֲסוּ הַבּוֹנִים,   הָיְתָה לְרֹאשׁ פִּנָּה.
אֶבֶן מָאֲסוּ הַבּוֹנִים,   הָיְתָה לְרֹאשׁ פִּנָּה.
מֵאֵת יְיָ הָיְתָה זֹּאת,   הִיא נִפְלָאת בְּעֵינֵינוּ.
מֵאֵת יְיָ הָיְתָה זֹּאת,   הִיא נִפְלָאת בְּעֵינֵינוּ.
זֶה הַיּוֹם עָשָׂה יְיָ,   נָגִילָה וְנִשְׂמְחָה בוֹ.
זֶה הַיּוֹם עָשָׂה יְיָ,   נָגִילָה וְנִשְׂמְחָה בוֹ.

אָנָּא יְיָ הוֹשִׁיעָה נָּא: אָנָּא יְיָ הוֹשִׁיעָה נָּא:
אָנָּא יְיָ הַצְלִיחָה נָּא: אָנָּא יְיָ הַצְלִיחָה נָּא:

בָּרוּךְ הַבָּא בְּשֵׁם יְיָ,   בֵּרַכְנוּכֶם מִבֵּית יְיָ.
בָּרוּךְ הַבָּא בְּשֵׁם יְיָ,   בֵּרַכְנוּכֶם מִבֵּית יְיָ.
אֵל יְיָ וַיָּאֶר לָנוּ,   אִסְרוּ חַג בַּעֲבֹתִים

עַד קַרְנוֹת הַמִּזְבֵּחַ.

אֵלִי אַתָּה וְאוֹדֶךָּ,   אֱלֹהַי אֲרוֹמְמֶךָּ.
הוֹדוּ לַיְיָ כִּי טוֹב,   כִּי לְעוֹלָם חַסְדּוֹ.

יְהַלְלוּךָ יְיָ אֱלֹהֵינוּ כָּל מַעֲשֶׂיךָ, וַחֲסִידֶיךָ צַדִּיקִים עוֹשֵׂי רְצוֹנֶךָ, וְכָל עַמְּךָ בֵּית יִשְׂרָאֵל בְּרִנָּה יוֹדוּ וִיבָרְכוּ וִישַׁבְּחוּ וִיפָאֲרוּ וִירוֹמְמוּ וְיַעֲרִיצוּ וְיַקְדִּישׁוּ וְיַמְלִיכוּ אֶת שִׁמְךָ מַלְכֵּנוּ, כִּי לְךָ טוֹב לְהוֹדוֹת וּלְשִׁמְךָ נָאֶה לְזַמֵּר, כִּי מֵעוֹלָם וְעַד עוֹלָם אַתָּה אֵל. בָּרוּךְ אַתָּה יְיָ, מֶלֶךְ מְהֻלָּל בַּתִּשְׁבָּחוֹת.

Count the Omer
(second night only)

Passover is both an historical festival celebrating the Exodus from Egypt and an agricultural holiday marking the beginning of the barley harvest.

On the second day of Passover, an *omer*, a sheath of barley, was brought to the Temple in Jerusalem as an offering. Shavuot comes forty-nine days later and marks the beginning of the wheat harvest.

Shavuot is also the time of the giving of the Torah. We count the forty-nine days to this festival to show the connection--that our freedom was not complete until we received the Torah. At Sinai, we switched our allegiance from a human ruler to becoming "servants of God."

(Count the omer with the blessing.)

בָּרוּךְ אַתָּה יי אֱלֹהֵינוּ מֶלֶךְ הָעוֹלָם אֲשֶׁר קִדְּשָׁנוּ בְּמִצְוֹתָיו וְצִוָּנוּ עַל סְפִירַת הָעֹמֶר.
הַיּוֹם יוֹם אֶחָד לָעֹמֶר.

Baruch Atah Adonai, Eloheinu melech haolam, asher kid'shanu b'mitzvotav, v'tzivanu al sefirat ha'omer. Hayom yom echad la'omer.

Blessed are You, Adonai our God, Sovereign of the world, who made us holy by Your mitzvot and commanded us to count the omer.

TODAY IS THE FIRST DAY OF THE OMER.

The seven weeks between Pesach and Shavuot were a period of great anxiety as the ancient Israelites awaited the wheat harvest. It was also a time of upheaval for them. They were living in a new place under new leadership, trying to understand what it meant to be a free people. We can reflect on this period of Jewish history as we count the omer, and we can also share stories of our own transitions.[34]

After the Exodus, the Israelites had to wait patiently for seven weeks to reach Mount Sinai. Some things are worth the wait!

THE ROSENSTEIN HAGGADAH

SEDER SONGS

Adir Hu (Mighty Is God) אַדִּיר הוּא

אַדִּיר הוּא, אַדִּיר הוּא, יִבְנֶה בֵיתוֹ בְּקָרוֹב, בִּמְהֵרָה בִּמְהֵרָה, בְּיָמֵינוּ בְּקָרוֹב. אֵל בְּנֵה, בְּנֵה בֵיתְךָ בְּקָרוֹב.

בָּחוּר הוּא, גָּדוֹל הוּא, דָּגוּל הוּא, יִבְנֶה בֵיתוֹ בְּקָרוֹב, בִּמְהֵרָה בִּמְהֵרָה, בְּיָמֵינוּ בְּקָרוֹב. אֵל בְּנֵה, אֵל בְּנֵה, בְּנֵה בֵיתְךָ בְּקָרוֹב.

הָדוּר הוּא, וָתִיק הוּא, זַכַּאי הוּא, חָסִיד הוּא, יִבְנֶה בֵיתוֹ בְּקָרוֹב, בִּמְהֵרָה בִּמְהֵרָה, בְּיָמֵינוּ בְּקָרוֹב. אֵל בְּנֵה, אֵל בְּנֵה, בְּנֵה בֵיתְךָ בְּקָרוֹב.

טָהוֹר הוּא, יָחִיד הוּא, כַּבִּיר הוּא, לָמוּד הוּא, מֶלֶךְ הוּא, נוֹרָא הוּא, סַגִּיב הוּא, עִזּוּז הוּא, פּוֹדֶה הוּא, צַדִּיק הוּא, יִבְנֶה בֵיתוֹ בְּקָרוֹב, בִּמְהֵרָה בִּמְהֵרָה, בְּיָמֵינוּ בְּקָרוֹב. אֵל בְּנֵה, אֵל בְּנֵה, בְּנֵה בֵיתְךָ בְּקָרוֹב.

קָדוֹשׁ הוּא, רַחוּם הוּא, שַׁדַּי הוּא, תַּקִּיף הוּא, יִבְנֶה בֵיתוֹ בְּקָרוֹב, בִּמְהֵרָה בִּמְהֵרָה, בְּיָמֵינוּ בְּקָרוֹב. אֵל בְּנֵה, אֵל בְּנֵה, בְּנֵה בֵיתְךָ בְּקָרוֹב.

Adir hu, adir hu, yivneh veito b'karov, bimheirah, bimheirah, b'yameinu b'karov. Eil b'nai, Eil b'nei, b'nei vetcha b'karov.

Bachur hu, gadol hu, dagul hu...
Hadur hu, vatik hu, zakai hu, chassid hu...
Tahor hu, yahid hu, kabir hu, lamud hu, melech hu...
Nora hu, sagiv hu, izuz hu, podeh hu, tzadik hu ...
Kadosh hu, rachum hu, shadai hu, takif hu...

Mighty is God
May God's kingdom be established speedily and in our lifetime.

God is chosen, great, renowned, glorious, faithful, just, pious, pure, unique, powerful, knowing, majestic, awesome, exalted, potent, redeeming, righteous, holy, merciful, sustaining, and forceful.

Adir Hu lists attributes of God following the Hebrew alphabet. Go around the room, each saying your own attribute, following the English alphabet. For example, Awesome is God, Blessed is God, Comforting is God and so forth.

THE ROSENSTEIN HAGGADAH

Echad Mi Yodea? ‏אֶחָד מִי יוֹדֵעַ?‏

‏אֶחָד מִי יוֹדֵעַ? אֶחָד אֲנִי יוֹדֵעַ: אֶחָד אֱלֹהֵינוּ שֶׁבַּשָּׁמַיִם וּבָאָרֶץ.‏

‏שְׁנַיִם מִי יוֹדֵעַ? שְׁנַיִם אֲנִי יוֹדֵעַ: שְׁנֵי לֻחוֹת הַבְּרִית, אֶחָד אֱלֹהֵינוּ שֶׁבַּשָּׁמַיִם וּבָאָרֶץ.‏

‏שְׁלֹשָׁה מִי יוֹדֵעַ? שְׁלֹשָׁה אֲנִי יוֹדֵעַ: שְׁלֹשָׁה אָבוֹת, שְׁנֵי לֻחוֹת הַבְּרִית, אֶחָד אֱלֹהֵינוּ שֶׁבַּשָּׁמַיִם וּבָאָרֶץ.‏

‏אַרְבַּע מִי יוֹדֵעַ? אַרְבַּע אֲנִי יוֹדֵעַ: אַרְבַּע אִמָּהוֹת, שְׁלֹשָׁה אָבוֹת, שְׁנֵי לֻחוֹת הַבְּרִית, אֶחָד אֱלֹהֵינוּ שֶׁבַּשָּׁמַיִם וּבָאָרֶץ.‏

‏חֲמִשָּׁה מִי יוֹדֵעַ? חֲמִשָּׁה אֲנִי יוֹדֵעַ: חֲמִשָּׁה חוּמְשֵׁי תוֹרָה, אַרְבַּע אִמָּהוֹת, שְׁלֹשָׁה אָבוֹת, שְׁנֵי לֻחוֹת הַבְּרִית, אֶחָד אֱלֹהֵינוּ שֶׁבַּשָּׁמַיִם וּבָאָרֶץ.‏

‏שִׁשָּׁה מִי יוֹדֵעַ? שִׁשָּׁה אֲנִי יוֹדֵעַ: שִׁשָּׁה סִדְרֵי מִשְׁנָה, חֲמִשָּׁה חוּמְשֵׁי תוֹרָה, אַרְבַּע אִמָּהוֹת, שְׁלֹשָׁה אָבוֹת, שְׁנֵי לֻחוֹת הַבְּרִית, אֶחָד אֱלֹהֵינוּ שֶׁבַּשָּׁמַיִם וּבָאָרֶץ.‏

‏שִׁבְעָה מִי יוֹדֵעַ? שִׁבְעָה אֲנִי יוֹדֵעַ: שִׁבְעָה יְמֵי שַׁבַּתָּא, שִׁשָּׁה סִדְרֵי מִשְׁנָה, חֲמִשָּׁה חוּמְשֵׁי תוֹרָה, אַרְבַּע אִמָּהוֹת, שְׁלֹשָׁה אָבוֹת, שְׁנֵי לֻחוֹת הַבְּרִית, אֶחָד אֱלֹהֵינוּ שֶׁבַּשָּׁמַיִם וּבָאָרֶץ.‏

‏שְׁמוֹנָה מִי יוֹדֵעַ? שְׁמוֹנָה אֲנִי יוֹדֵעַ: שְׁמוֹנָה יְמֵי מִילָה, שִׁבְעָה יְמֵי שַׁבַּתָּא, שִׁשָּׁה סִדְרֵי מִשְׁנָה, חֲמִשָּׁה חוּמְשֵׁי תוֹרָה, אַרְבַּע אִמָּהוֹת, שְׁלֹשָׁה אָבוֹת, שְׁנֵי לֻחוֹת הַבְּרִית, אֶחָד אֱלֹהֵינוּ שֶׁבַּשָּׁמַיִם וּבָאָרֶץ.‏

‏תִּשְׁעָה מִי יוֹדֵעַ? תִּשְׁעָה אֲנִי יוֹדֵעַ: תִּשְׁעָה יַרְחֵי לֵדָה, שְׁמוֹנָה יְמֵי מִילָה, שִׁבְעָה יְמֵי שַׁבַּתָּא, שִׁשָּׁה סִדְרֵי מִשְׁנָה, חֲמִשָּׁה חוּמְשֵׁי תוֹרָה, אַרְבַּע אִמָּהוֹת, שְׁלֹשָׁה אָבוֹת, שְׁנֵי לֻחוֹת הַבְּרִית, אֶחָד אֱלֹהֵינוּ שֶׁבַּשָּׁמַיִם וּבָאָרֶץ.‏

‏עֲשָׂרָה מִי יוֹדֵעַ? עֲשָׂרָה אֲנִי יוֹדֵעַ: עֲשָׂרָה דִבְּרַיָּא, תִּשְׁעָה יַרְחֵי לֵדָה, שְׁמוֹנָה יְמֵי מִילָה, שִׁבְעָה יְמֵי שַׁבַּתָּא, שִׁשָּׁה סִדְרֵי מִשְׁנָה, חֲמִשָּׁה חוּמְשֵׁי תוֹרָה, אַרְבַּע אִמָּהוֹת, שְׁלֹשָׁה אָבוֹת, שְׁנֵי לֻחוֹת הַבְּרִית, אֶחָד אֱלֹהֵינוּ שֶׁבַּשָּׁמַיִם וּבָאָרֶץ.‏

‏אַחַד עָשָׂר מִי יוֹדֵעַ? אַחַד עָשָׂר אֲנִי יוֹדֵעַ: אַחַד עָשָׂר כּוֹכְבַיָּא, עֲשָׂרָה דִבְּרַיָּא, תִּשְׁעָה יַרְחֵי לֵדָה, שְׁמוֹנָה יְמֵי מִילָה, שִׁבְעָה יְמֵי שַׁבַּתָּא, שִׁשָּׁה סִדְרֵי מִשְׁנָה, חֲמִשָּׁה חוּמְשֵׁי תוֹרָה, אַרְבַּע אִמָּהוֹת, שְׁלֹשָׁה אָבוֹת, שְׁנֵי לֻחוֹת הַבְּרִית, אֶחָד אֱלֹהֵינוּ שֶׁבַּשָּׁמַיִם וּבָאָרֶץ.‏

‏שְׁנֵים עָשָׂר מִי יוֹדֵעַ? שְׁנֵים עָשָׂר אֲנִי יוֹדֵעַ: שְׁנֵים עָשָׂר שִׁבְטַיָּא, אַחַד עָשָׂר כּוֹכְבַיָּא, עֲשָׂרָה דִבְּרַיָּא, תִּשְׁעָה יַרְחֵי לֵדָה, שְׁמוֹנָה יְמֵי מִילָה, שִׁבְעָה יְמֵי שַׁבַּתָּא, שִׁשָּׁה סִדְרֵי מִשְׁנָה, חֲמִשָּׁה חוּמְשֵׁי תוֹרָה, אַרְבַּע אִמָּהוֹת, שְׁלֹשָׁה אָבוֹת, שְׁנֵי לֻחוֹת הַבְּרִית, אֶחָד אֱלֹהֵינוּ שֶׁבַּשָּׁמַיִם וּבָאָרֶץ.‏

‏שְׁלֹשָׁה עָשָׂר מִי יוֹדֵעַ? שְׁלֹשָׁה עָשָׂר אֲנִי יוֹדֵעַ: שְׁלֹשָׁה עָשָׂר מִדַּיָּא, שְׁנֵים עָשָׂר שִׁבְטַיָּא, אַחַד עָשָׂר כּוֹכְבַיָּא, עֲשָׂרָה דִבְּרַיָּא, תִּשְׁעָה יַרְחֵי לֵדָה, שְׁמוֹנָה יְמֵי מִילָה, שִׁבְעָה יְמֵי שַׁבַּתָּא, שִׁשָּׁה סִדְרֵי מִשְׁנָה, חֲמִשָּׁה חוּמְשֵׁי תוֹרָה, אַרְבַּע אִמָּהוֹת, שְׁלֹשָׁה אָבוֹת, שְׁנֵי לֻחוֹת הַבְּרִית, אֶחָד אֱלֹהֵינוּ שֶׁבַּשָּׁמַיִם וּבָאָרֶץ.‏

Echad Mi Yodea?
Who Knows One?

(As you sing each new verse, add the ones you previously sang.)

Echad Mi Yodea?

Echad mi yodea? Echad ani yodea!
Echad Eloheinu, sh'bashamayim uva'aretz

Shnei luchot habrit, shlosha avot, arba imahot, chamisha chumshei Torah, shisha sidrei Mishna, shiv'ah y'mai shabata, shmonah y'mai milah, tishah yarchei leidah, asarah debraiyah, achad asar kochvaiya, shenem asar shivtaiya, shlosha asar midaiya

Who Knows One?

Who knows 1?	I know 1!	One is our God in the heaven and earth.
Who knows 2?	I know 2!	There are 2 tablets of the law.
Who knows 3?	I know 3!	There are 3 fathers.
Who knows 4?	I know 4!	There are 4 mothers.
Who knows 5?	I know 5!	There are 5 books of the Torah.
Who knows 6?	I know 6!	There are 6 books of Mishna.
Who knows 7?	I know 7!	There are 7 days of the week.
Who knows 8?	I know 8!	There are 8 days to circumcision.
Who knows 9?	I know 9!	There are 9 months of pregnancy.
Who knows 10?	I know 10!	There are 10 commandments.
Who knows 11?	I know 11!	There are 11 stars in Joseph's dream.
Who knows 12?	I know 12!	There are 12 tribes.
Who knows 13?	I know 13!	There are 13 attributes of God.

Echad Mi Yodea (Who Knows One?) is a most appropriate song to sing, as this is a night of numbers and calculations. The song also enumerates the basic elements of our faith and tradition. The song has a special appeal to children. It is also an opportunity for them to show off their knowledge by answering, "I know one" etc.

Ask a different participant to answer each question. As the song repeats, each says his or her part. Add motions to add to the fun.

Chad Gadya חַד גַּדְיָא
(One Only Kid)

(As you add each character, repeat all that has thus far been sung, so the song increases with each verse, whether in Hebrew or English. Add the chorus after each verse.)

חַד גַּדְיָא, חַד גַּדְיָא
דְּזַבִּין אַבָּא בִּתְרֵי זוּזֵי, חַד
גַּדְיָא, חַד גַּדְיָא.

וְאָתָא שׁוּנְרָא, וְאָכְלָה לְגַדְיָא,
דְּזַבִּין אַבָּא בִּתְרֵי זוּזֵי, חַד
גַּדְיָא, חַד גַּדְיָא.

וְאָתָא כַלְבָּא, וְנָשַׁךְ לְשׁוּנְרָא,
דְּאָכְלָה לְגַדְיָא, דְּזַבִּין אַבָּא
בִּתְרֵי זוּזֵי, חַד גַּדְיָא, חַד גַּדְיָא.

וְאָתָא חוּטְרָא, וְהִכָּה לְכַלְבָּא,
דְּנָשַׁךְ לְשׁוּנְרָא, דְּאָכְלָה
לְגַדְיָא, דְּזַבִּין אַבָּא בִּתְרֵי זוּזֵי,
חַד גַּדְיָא, חַד גַּדְיָא.

וְאָתָא נוּרָא, וְשָׂרַף לְחוּטְרָא,
דְּהִכָּה לְכַלְבָּא, דְּנָשַׁךְ
לְשׁוּנְרָא, דְּאָכְלָה לְגַדְיָא,
דְּזַבִּין אַבָּא בִּתְרֵי זוּזֵי, חַד
גַּדְיָא, חַד גַּדְיָא.

וְאָתָא מַיָּא, וְכָבָה לְנוּרָא,
דְּשָׂרַף לְחוּטְרָא, דְּהִכָּה
לְכַלְבָּא, דְּנָשַׁךְ לְשׁוּנְרָא,
דְּאָכְלָה לְגַדְיָא, דְּזַבִּין אַבָּא
בִּתְרֵי זוּזֵי, חַד גַּדְיָא, חַד
גַּדְיָא.   וְאָתָא תוֹרָא, וְשָׁתָא
לְמַיָּא, דְּכָבָה לְנוּרָא, דְּשָׂרַף
לְחוּטְרָא, דְּהִכָּה לְכַלְבָּא,
דְּנָשַׁךְ לְשׁוּנְרָא, דְּאָכְלָה
לְגַדְיָא, דְּזַבִּין אַבָּא בִּתְרֵי זוּזֵי,
חַד גַּדְיָא, חַד גַּדְיָא.

וְאָתָא הַשּׁוֹחֵט, וְשָׁחַט לְתוֹרָא,
דְּשָׁתָא לְמַיָּא, דְּכָבָה לְנוּרָא,
דְּשָׂרַף לְחוּטְרָא, דְּהִכָּה
לְכַלְבָּא, דְּנָשַׁךְ לְשׁוּנְרָא,
דְּאָכְלָה לְגַדְיָא, דְּזַבִּין אַבָּא
בִּתְרֵי זוּזֵי, חַד גַּדְיָא, חַד גַּדְיָא.

וְאָתָא מַלְאַךְ הַמָּוֶת, וְשָׁחַט
לְשׁוֹחֵט, דְּשָׁחַט לְתוֹרָא,
דְּשָׁתָא לְמַיָּא, דְּכָבָה לְנוּרָא,
דְּשָׂרַף לְחוּטְרָא, דְּהִכָּה
לְכַלְבָּא, דְּנָשַׁךְ לְשׁוּנְרָא,
דְּאָכְלָה לְגַדְיָא, דְּזַבִּין אַבָּא
בִּתְרֵי זוּזֵי, חַד גַּדְיָא, חַד גַּדְיָא.

וְאָתָא הַקָּדוֹשׁ בָּרוּךְ הוּא,
וְשָׁחַט לְמַלְאַךְ הַמָּוֶת, דְּשָׁחַט
לְתוֹרָא, דְּשָׁתָא לְמַיָּא, דְּכָבָה
לְנוּרָא, דְּשָׂרַף לְחוּטְרָא,
דְּהִכָּה לְכַלְבָּא, דְּנָשַׁךְ
לְשׁוּנְרָא, דְּאָכְלָה לְגַדְיָא,
דְּזַבִּין אַבָּא בִּתְרֵי זוּזֵי, חַד
גַּדְיָא, חַד גַּדְיָא.

Chad Gadya

Introduction
**Chad Gadya, chad Gadya
D'zabin abba bit'trei zuzei,
Chad Gadya, chad Gadya.**

Chorus
**D'zabin abba bit'rei zuzei
Chad Gadya, chad gadya.**

One Only Kid

Introduction
One only kid, one only kid
that my father bought for two zuzim.
One only kid, one only kid.

Chorus
that my father bought for two zuzim.
One only kid, one only kid.

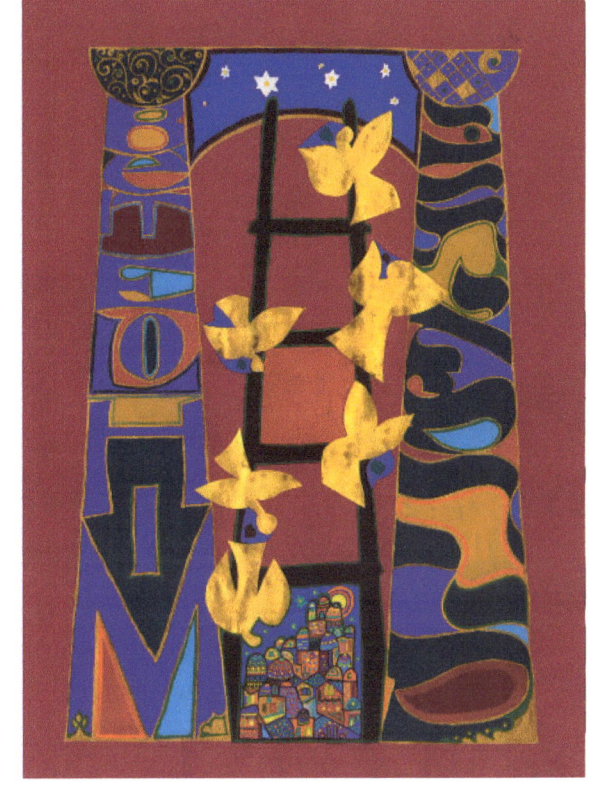

Along came a cat and ate the kid…
Along came a dog and bit the cat…
Along came a stick and beat the dog…
Along came a fire and burnt the stick…
Along came water and put out the fire…
Along came an ox and drank the water…
Along came a butcher and slaughtered the ox…
Along came the angel of death and slew the butcher…
Along came the Holy One and killed the angel of death…

In this song, written in Aramaic, the Jewish people is compared to an innocent young goat that the parent bought for two zuzim, which stands for the Ten Commandments, (the two tablets of the law.) We are set upon by many enemies---the cat is Assyria, the dog is Babylonia, the stick is Persia, the fire is Greece, the water is Rome, the ox is the Saracens, the butcher is the crusaders, and the angel of death is the Ottoman empire. In the end, they devour each other. The song concludes with the expression of hope that evil will be overcome and God will bring about a safe and peaceful world.

We sing the song quickly because we don't want to dwell on the bad, but want to reach the happy ending. The last verse is traditionally sung slowly.

L'shana Haba'ah B'Yerushalyim—Interpretations

- For traditional Jews, when Messiah comes, Jerusalem and the rebuilt Temple will be the focal point of our people.
- For many non-traditional Jews, saying the verse emphasizes their continued support for the State of Israel, as well as their ties to its culture and people.
- Others hope for a peaceful Jerusalem and pray that Israel will continue to be a potential safe haven for diaspora Jews.
- There are those who see Jerusalem as representing our spiritual redemption.
- Jerusalem can also stand for our ideal society, reflecting our values and visions.[35]

What do you express when you sing this verse?

NIRTZAH

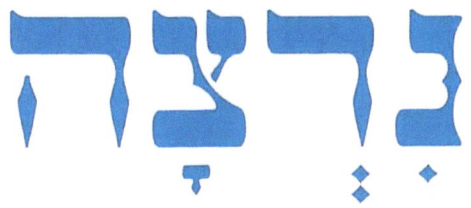

COMPLETE THE SEDER

The Fourth Cup – "I Will Take You To Be My People"

We are now ready for the fourth cup of wine, which we drink while reclining.
Baruch Atah Adonai, Eloheinu melech haolam, borei p'ree ha gafen.

בָּרוּךְ אַתָּה יְיָ, אֱלֹהֵינוּ מֶלֶךְ הָעוֹלָם, בּוֹרֵא פְּרִי הַגָּפֶן:

Blessed are You Adonai, Sovereign of the world, who creates the fruit of the vine.

(Drink the fourth cup while reclining.)

Chasal siddur Pesach k'hilchato	חֲסַל סִדּוּר פֶּסַח כְּהִלְכָתוֹ,
K'chol mishpato v'chukato.	כְּכָל מִשְׁפָּטוֹ וְחֻקָּתוֹ.
Ka'asher zachinu l'sader oto	כַּאֲשֶׁר זָכִינוּ לְסַדֵּר אוֹתוֹ,
Ken nizkeh la'asoto.	כֵּן נִזְכֶּה לַעֲשׂוֹתוֹ.
Zach shochen m'onah	זָךְ שׁוֹכֵן מְעוֹנָה,
Komem k'hal adat mi manah.	קוֹמֵם קְהַל עֲדַת מִי מָנָה.
B'karov nahel nitei chanah	בְּקָרוֹב נַהֵל נִטְעֵי כַנָּה,
P'duyim l'Zion b'rina.	פְּדוּיִם לְצִיּוֹן בְּרִנָּה.

The Passover Seder can set the tone for one's spirituality throughout the year. Thus we pray that all we have arranged for this night, all of our spiritual plantings, will bear fruit.

Our Seder is now completed. We have fulfilled every law and custom from our tradition. As we celebrated this year, may we be granted the blessing of celebrating Passover for many years to come. We pray to You, Pure and Holy One, Transcendent and Immanent God, to raise up your people with love and lead us to Zion in joyful song.

L'shana haba'ah b'Yerushalayim!

In our time, some suggest that we drink a fifth cup of wine to celebrate the establishment of The State of Israel. It is an appropriate time to sing Hatikvah, the Jewish National Anthem.

Hatikvah   הַתִּקְוָה

כָּל־עוֹד בַּלֵּבָב פְּנִימָה, נֶפֶשׁ יְהוּדִי הוֹמִיָּה,
וּלְפַאֲתֵי מִזְרָח קָדִימָה, עַיִן לְצִיּוֹן צוֹפִיָּה.
עוֹד לֹא אָבְדָה תִקְוָתֵנוּ, הַתִּקְוָה בַּת שְׁנוֹת אַלְפַּיִם
לִהְיוֹת עַם חָפְשִׁי בְּאַרְצֵנוּ, אֶרֶץ צִיּוֹן וִירוּשָׁלַיִם.

Kol od balevav p'nimah, Nefesh Yehudi homiyah.
Ul'fatei mizrach kadimah, Ayin l'tzion tzofiyah.
Od lo avdah tikvatenu, Hatikvah, bat sh'not alpayim
Li'yot am chofshi b'artzenu, Eretz Tzion V'Yerushalyim.
(Repeat last two lines)

The words to Hatikvah, (Israel's national anthem), were written in 1886 by Naphtali Herz Imber. Imber was born in Zloczow (now Zolochiv, Ukraine) a city that was part of the Austro-Hungarian Empire. He began writing poems at the age of ten and in his later years was given an award by Emperor Franz Joseph for a poem he wrote. He immigrated to Ottoman Palestine in 1882 and published Hatikvah in 1886, based on an earlier poem he had written. He spent his later years in London, Chicago and New York, where he was buried. Imber was re-interred in a cemetery in Jerusalem.

The melody for Hatikvah, has generally been credited to Samuel Cohen, an immigrant from Moldavia. In 1888, he composed a melody based on a Romanian folk song. The melody was a modification of a 17th century Italian composition called, La Montovana. La Montovana was also modified a few years before Cohen, by Czech composer Bedrich Smetana in his piece, "Die Molda." There is a strong resemblance between the two pieces. There has been a dispute, with some crediting Nissan Belzer, a cantor from Beltz in the Ukraine, as the composer.[36]

Hatikvah - The Hope

As long as deep in our hearts,
 A Jewish soul still yearns,
With eyes turned Eastward
To Jerusalem, to Zion,
Then our hope is not lost
A two thousand year old hope:
To be a free people in our land,
The land of Zion and Jerusalem.

Closing Thoughts

As we close our Haggadot, we pray that we may be granted the passion and dedication to work for freedom and peace, as so many have done before us.

END NOTES

1. This information was posted on the women's tefillah network listserv 4/10/01, by Rabbi Sue Fendrick, with permission of professor Susannah Heschel, who created the "orange ritual" as a symbol of GLBTQ inclusion in the Jewish community.

2. Miriam Hyman, CAJECURRICULUM BANK, p. 8.

3. FAMILYLINK, ACAJE, Philadelphia, 2006.

4. Ruth Feldstein, Passover Seder Exchange, Jewish Centre, Princeton, 1987.

5. failedmessiah.com

6. Shoshana Silberman, A Family Haggadah, Karben, Rockville, MD, 1987 (revised edition Lerner Publishing Group, Minneapolis, 2007.) p. 13.

7. FamilyLink , ACAJE Philadelphia, 2006

8. mochajuden.com p 3.

9. Bridgette Dayan, Shema, June, 2004.

10. Pesach With Pizazz, Supplement for Families, Department of Education, Jewish Federation of Southern New Jersey, 2001.

11. Rabbi Annie Tucker, The Four Children Seder, Supplement for Congregants, Jewish Centre, Princeton, 2012.

12. Philip Goodman, Passover Anthology, Jewish Publication Society, Philadelphia, 1966 pp. 407-408.

13. Tamara Cohen, Rabbi Sue Levi Elwell, & Ronni M. Horn. Ma'ayan Haggadah. New York. 2001. P26.

14. Rabbi Marc Angel, A Sephardic Seder, Ktav, Hoboken, 1998. p.13.

15. rahelsjewishindia.com p. 8.

16. whyisthisnight.com/customs.html

17. Website: Seder Customs Around The World

18. My Jewish Learning 2013.

19. Haggadah The Passover Story, Gerard Garouste & Marc-Alain Quaknin, Assouline Publishing Company, Inc. New York, 2001, p. 87.

20. Jeffrey M. Cohen, 1001 Questions & Answers on Pesach, Jason Aronson, Northdale, NJ. pp. 110-111.

21. A teaching of Rav Soleveichik, in Exile To Redemption, compiled by Rabbi Alter Eliyou Freidman & Uri Kaploun, Chabad,1993, p.64.

22. mochajuden.com

23. Nosson Sherman & Meir Zlotowitz, Abarbanel Haggadah, Mesorah Publishing Company, 1990, p. 35.

24. Jonathan Sachs, Rabbi Jonathan Sach's Haggadah, Continuum, New York, 2016, p.15.

25. Rabbi Aryeh Kaplan, Innerspace: Introduction to Kabblah, Meditation and Prophecy, Moznaim Publishing Company, Brooklyn, 1990, p. 160.

26. JewishAnswers.org

27. I originally learned this custom from Rabbi Jeff Schein. Now my Iranian nephew by marriage, leads this at our Seder.

28. Aviva Zornberg, The Particulars of Rapture, Schocken, New York, 2001.

29. Medieval French commentator Rashi

30. Rabbi Naphtali of Rephiz

31. Top 50 Passover Traditions from Around the World, huffingtonpost.com

32. Rabbi David Golinkin, ASK.COM

33. belief.net Unique Passover Traditions

34. This commentary was part of a farewell letter by Rabbi Annie Tucker to our congregation –The Jewish Centre, Princeton NJ. (We still miss her!)

35. Michele Alperin. Next year In Jerusalem, MyJewishlwarning.com 2005.

36. Times of Israel website, March 2018

ART NOTES

Created by Mordechai Rosenstein

HOME between Dedication and Introduction pages
The bright orange light means welcome.

ZODIAC page 4
The signs of the Zodiac are universal and ancient. The Talmud speaks of them in a good fashion. At least one ancient synagogue in Israel has been found with the zodiac done in mosaic on the synagogue floor.

GOODNESS page 9
Plant, harvest immediately suggests green. I used this color for the Hebrew words to strengthen the images, sow and reap in joy.

THIS IS THE DAY page 10
The letters form words but they are very abstract when used here. Night and day are expressed in the circle of the heavenly bodies, sun, moon and stars.

EXODUS page 12
This painting references the parting of the waters, the giving of the Torah, and the beginning of our people as a nation.

WINE page 13
All of our good times begin with a little wine.

THE WATERS WERE SPLIT page 17
What a mighty time!

SEASONS page 18
"For everything there is a season and a time for every purpose under heaven."

BELOVED page 19
Solomon's Song of Songs has provided generations of lovers with the words to say, "I love you."

GOD SPOKE TO MOSES page 25
Here we are reminded that the Torah was given to us by the Creator, through his faithful servant Moses.

NARROW BRIDGE page 26
"All the world is a narrow bridge; but the important thing is not to be afraid." This teaching by Reb Nachman is good advice for all of us on the journey of life. Notice the narrow bridge, but help going forward.

SHEMA (Listen) page 27
"Hear O' Israel" is recited morning and night. The Menorah is outside the Israeli K'nesset in Jerusalem.

SHADDAI (God) page 29
Shaddai is one of the names of the Creator. The "Almighty", the Power, eclipses the sun, and can be found in the simple letter "Yud", which the rabbis say can be found in every letter of the alphabet.

THE ROSENSTEIN HAGGADAH

EDUCATION page 31
" Show a child the way he/she should go." The result of this is that the child becomes (from bottom to top) knowledgeable, has love of Torah and attains the crown of a good name.

TURN IT page 32
We are instructed to turn it and turn it, as all our ancestors can be found in it.

HILLEL page 33
Hillel's teaching seems to have summed it all up for the direction of our lives. It is universal and just.

THE LORD IS MY LIGHT page 36
The first act of creation was the light brought forth by the Creator.

LEARNING page 38
"To Learn and To Teach" is a calligrapher's dream – so many "Lameds", my favorite letter. It maintains its identity, which artistically permits it to be used creatively in so many ways.

MI CHAMOCHA. (Who is Like You, God) page 39
The waters have parted. The sea is crossed. And the Torah is given on Mt. Sinai. "Who is like unto You in all the heavens, our God!"

JUSTICE page 40
We are commanded twice to seek justice.

GET WISDOM page 41
Wisdom and understanding are a solid foundation and are expressed in the design structure.

FIVE BOOKS page 43
Bereshit - One day, "Let there be light."
Sh'mot – parting of the sea and giving of the Torah
Vayikra – Israel camped around the Mishkan and traveled for forty years
Bamidbar – Moses is preparing the people for new leadership (Joshuah) and coined the phrase, "Go west young man, go west!" Cross the Jordan and claim the Promised Land.
D'varim – reviews it all

REMEMBER page 44
We are promised that God's covenant with the children of Israel will be unbroken.

SIMCHA (Joy) page 46
It is good to express joy in life's every opportunity.

FOLLOW ME page 47
This is a piece to memorialize Michael Levin (zl"), a lone soldier, killed in the Lebanon War in 2006. "Follow me" is the call of every Israeli leader in battle. Michael was raised in Bucks County, PA and attended Camp Ramah. He was also active in USY.

HINENI (Here I am.) page 49
Notice the cursive "Heh" at the bottom of the word. As we answer, " Hineni, Here I am", we rise to a higher purpose and the letters slowly become more refined, reaching the perfect "Yud" form.

GENERATION TO GENERATION page 50
Notice that "Daled" and "Resh" are very very similar. Thank God for the "Lamed" to give me some movement and excitement.

THE ROSENSTEIN HAGGADAH

KING DAVID page 51
This is my image of King David, the "sweet singer of Israel." The harp image was drawn with a Chinese lettering brush, done in just a few strokes.

TRUST page 54
I find much interest in other alphabet forms. Here, the English letters are my inspired version of the famous, beautiful Irish prayer book, "The Book of Kells."

WATERS page 55
Notice how the letters form a large wave coming towards us, topped by white breakers. (I hope I achieved that effect.) This piece was created in CA in a Temple near the ocean.

OPEN YOUR HAND page 59
The psalms praise the Creator and to me, they are a bottomless well of visual inspiration.

CHAZAK (STRENGTH) page 61
Notice the Torah scroll. When a reading of a Book of the Torah is completed, the congregation in unison says, "Be strong, and let us strengthen each other."

WOMAN OF VALOR page 66
The Land of Knowledge represents the teaching of our mothers from birth. The necklace with twenty-two pearls represents the twenty-two vessels in Proverbs. "A woman of valor…etc." in alphabetical order. The word "woman" represents a crown of wisdom, dignity and understanding.

HALLELUYAH HORN page 68
"Proclaim Halleluyah with trumpet and timbrel." After crossing the Sea of Reeds, Miriam and the women went out with their timbrels and danced. Miriam announced, "Sing to God!" Sh'mot 15:20-21

ECHAD (One) page 75
When we recite the Shema, we bear witness to the fact that God is One. The "Ayin" is from the first word, and is enlarged, as is the "Daled" of the last word, "Echad." The two letters form the word in Hebrew for "witness."

HOUSE OF GOD page 79
Jacob arose from his dream of the angels climbing up and down a ladder. He exclaimed, "This is none other than the house of God!" (Genesis 28:17. The rabbis tell us that this was the Temple Mount. The two columns represent a distinctive feature of the first Temple.

STRANGER page 80
The commandment (to treat the stranger well, as you were once strangers in Egypt.) appears in the Torah more times than any other.

JERUSALEM OF THE MIND page 82
I could do a new image every day, inspired by our eternal capital Jerusalem.

CHAMSA (Five) page 84
This is an image representing the raised hands of the Kohanim (priests) as they bless us. It is a fifteen- word blessing ending in the word "peace" (Shalom.) Notice the similarity to the universal good luck symbol of the hand called "Chamsa."

ANNNOUNCE PEACE page 85
This is a beautiful vision of the prophet Isaiah. The blessing ends with the word "peace" – "shalom."